Paper Crafts
WORKSHOP

Paper Crafts
WORKSHOP

A Beginner's Guide
to Techniques & Projects

MARIE BROWNING

Sterling Publishing Co., Inc.
New York

Prolific Impressions Production Staff:

Editor in Chief: Mickey Baskett
Copy Editor: Phyllis Mueller
Graphics: Dianne Miller, Karen Turpin
Styling: Lenos Key
Photography: Jerry Mucklow of Rocket Photography, Visions West Photography
Administration: Jim Baskett

Library of Congress Cataloging-in-Publication Data Available

2 4 6 8 10 9 7 5 3 1

Published by Sterling Publishing Co., Inc.
387 Park Avenue South, New York, NY 10016
©2007 by Prolific Impressions, Inc.
Distributed in Canada by Sterling Publishing
c/o Canadian Manda Group, 165 Dufferin Street,
Toronto, Ontario, Canada M6K 3H6
Distributed in the United Kingdom by GMC Distribution Services,
Castle Place, 166 High Street, Lewes, East Sussex, England BN7 1XU
Distributed in Australia by Capricorn Link (Australia) Pty. Ltd.
P.O. Box 704, Windsor, NSW 2756, Australia

Printed in China

ISBN-13: 978-1-4027-3508-0
ISBN-10: 1-4027-3508-1

For information about custom editions, special sales, premium and corporate purchases, please contact Sterling Special Sales Department at 800-805-5489 or specialsales@sterlingpub.com.

Acknowledgments

I thank these manufacturers for their generous contributions of quality products and support in the creation of the projects.

For swirl flower rubber stamps, paper sculpture tools: Coronado Island Designs, Coronado, CA, www.cistamping.com

For two-part polymer coating (Envirotex-Lite), plastic measuring cups, disposable brushes, stir sticks, thin-bodied glue (Ultra-Seal): Environmental Technology Inc., Fields Landing, CA, www.eti-usa.com

For cutting tools, Cloud 9 Design decorative papers, and scrapbook embellishments and stickers: Fiskars Brands, Inc., Wausau, WI, www.fiskars.com

For decorative buttons, charms, and beads: Jesse James & Co. Allentown, PA, www.dressitup.com

For decorative papers, scrapbook embellishments, and stickers: K & Company Parkville, MO, www.kandcompany.com

For acrylic paints, Royal Coat decoupage mediums, decoupage prints, laser cut images and tools, acrylic varnishes, and dimensional varnish: Plaid Enterprises Inc., Norcross, GA, www.plaidonline.com

For paper craft and quilling supplies: Quilled Creations Penfield, NY, www.quilledcreations.com

About the Author

MARIE BROWNING

Marie Browning is a consummate craft designer who has made a career of designing products, writing books and articles, and teaching and demonstrating. You may have been charmed by her creative acumen but not been aware of the woman behind it; she has designed stencils, stamps, transfers, and a variety of other award-winning product lines for art and craft supply companies. As well as writing numerous books on creative living, Marie's articles and designs have appeared in numerous home decor and crafts magazines.

Marie Browning earned a Fine Arts Diploma from Camosun College and attended the University of Victoria. She is a member of the Crafts and Hobby Association (CHA). In 2004 Marie was selected by *Craftrends* (a trade publication) as a "Top Influential Industry Designer."

She lives, gardens, and crafts on Vancouver Island in Canada. She and her husband Scott have three children: Katelyn, Lena, and Jonathan. Marie can be contacted at www.mariebrowning.com

STERLING BOOKS BY MARIE BROWNING

Paper Crafts Workshop: Traditional Card Techniques (2007)

Metal Crafting Workshop (2006)

Casting for Crafters (2006)

Paper Mosaics in an Afternoon (2006)

Snazzy Jars (2006)

Jazzy Gift Baskets (2006)

Purse Pizzazz (2005)

Really Jazzy Jars (2005)

Totally Cool Polymer Clay for Kids (2005)

Totally Cool Soapmaking for Kids (2004 – reprinted in softcover)

Wonderful Wraps (2003 – reprinted in softcover)

Jazzy Jars (2003 – reprinted in softcover)

Designer Soapmaking (2003 – reprinted in German)

300 Recipes for Soap (2002 – reprinted in softcover and in French and Chinese)

Crafting with Vellum & Parchment (2001 – reprinted in softcover with the title *New Paper Crafts*)

Melt & Pour Soapmaking (2000 – reprinted in softcover)

Hand Decorating Paper (2000 – reprinted in softcover)

Memory Gifts (2000 – reprinted in softcover with the title *Family Photocrafts*)

Making Glorious Gifts from Your Garden (1999 – reprinted in softcover)

Handcrafted Journals, Albums, Scrapbooks & More (1999 – reprinted in softcover)

Beautiful Handmade Natural Soaps (1998 – reprinted in softcover with the title *Natural Soapmaking*)

Table of Contents

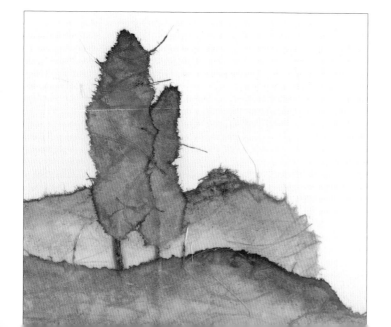

Welcome to Paper Crafting

There is almost nothing that can't be done with paper. Because the field of paper crafting is so broad, I've chosen to introduce the topic by showing you some basic techniques like cutting and folding and by presenting more detailed information about four different traditional paper crafting techniques: Collage, Quilling, Paper Tole, and Chigiri-e.

Collage, also often referred to as "altered art" includes traditional paper layering, tissue paper collage (made with bleeding tissue paper), and beeswax collage (where melted beeswax is used instead of glue). Collage can be used to decorate cards, scrapbook pages, home decor items, and journal pages.

Quilling is a traditional paper craft enjoying a renaissance with the introduction of exciting new papers (easy to find on the Internet). Incorporating sculptured paper flowers into quilled designs offers new creative opportunities. I have included simple projects that are quick and easy to make so you can learn this fun, inexpensive hobby.

Creating three-dimensional paper tole has never been so easy. New adhesives and ready-to-mount laser-cut images give the art of paper tole a brand new look that is quick and easy to attain. Scrapbook papers, greeting cards, and stickers are other sources of images you can use.

Chigiri-e is an ancient Japanese craft that uses torn paper pieces to create the look of beautiful watercolor paintings with fine handmade papers. Chigiri-e and its cut-paper cousin kiri-e are easy techniques to master. I show you how to color your own paper shapes for greater design flexibility.

In this book, you'll find information and photographs about the supplies and tools you need for each type of paper craft, along with numerous examples. You'll learn as you create beautiful cards, fun gift tags and packages, colorful wall pieces, decorative tabletop accents, and distinctive jewelry and purses.

Have fun learning or re-discovering these traditional paper crafts!

Marie Browning

Cutting Tools

Cutting tools are essential for all types of paper crafts. Sharp art knives and paper trimmers are used to cut papers to size for projects (scissors won't give you straight, sharp edges). Make sure you have a supply of additional blades for your cutting tools to ensure you'll always have a sharp edge.

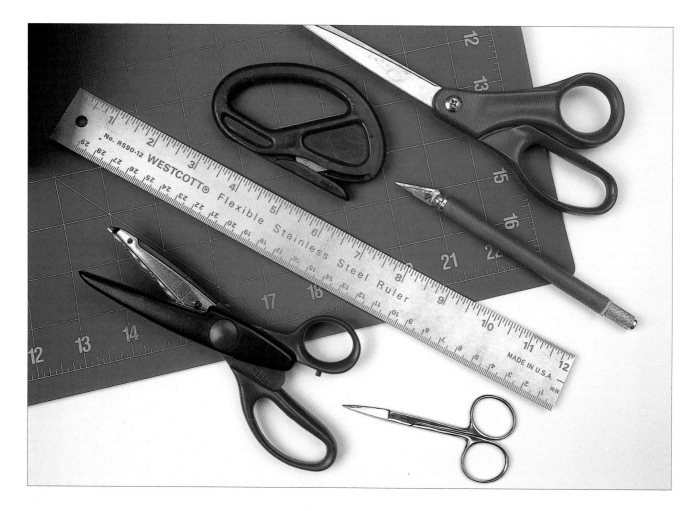

Art Knife

A scalpel-type **craft knife or art knife** with a replaceable, pointed blade is essential. It is an all-purpose cutting knife.

Paper Trimmer

A **paper trimmer** with a sliding blade makes cutting much easier and faster. A paper trimmer is excellent for cutting precise strips for paper weaving and for creating your own double-sided tape from double-sided adhesive sheets. You can find one in office supply catalogs and at crafts stores.

Scissors

Sharp **craft scissors** are needed for cutting small pieces, decorative treatments such as ribbons, and labels. Small sharp scissors are also used for cutting out images for three-dimensional effects.

Decorative edge scissors are available in a wide range of styles to give just the right finishing touch or creative edge. They can also be used to create lacy cutouts on pleated items such as fans and candle shades.

Cutting Mat

A **self-healing cutting mat** with a printed grid protects your work surface and aids accurate cutting. The mat's surface seals itself after each cut, so your knife won't follow a previous cut. Mats with 1", 1/2", and 1/4" grid marks make measuring and cutting perfectly square corners a breeze. Cutting mats range in size from 9" x 12" to sizes that will cover an entire tabletop. Buy the biggest mat your budget will allow.

Ruler

A straight-edge **metal ruler** with a cork backing is needed for perfectly straight cuts. Wooden and plastic rulers will slide and your knife will cut into them. It's useful to have a selection of lengths from 12" to 18".

CUTTING TECHNIQUES

Cutting is an important skill when working with paper, and many people cut incorrectly. Here are some tips on cutting with an art knife:

• Always measure twice and cut once.

• Use the grid markings on your cutting mat for measuring and lining up the paper. That way, you won't need to mark your paper, and your corners will be perfectly square.

• The key to successful cutting with an art or craft knife is a sharp blade. Always have extra blades handy to keep the knife in top cutting form. It is safer to use a sharp blade than a dull blade – a dull one can easily slip.

• Hold the art knife like a pen, with your index finger (it's your strongest) on top. You make cleaner cuts by exerting a downward pressure on the blade while cutting.

• Make sure the blade is held at a constant, low angle to the paper. Make strong, one-motion cuts towards you. If you press too hard, you will drag and rip the paper.

• When cutting with your metal ruler, hold the ruler down firmly with your non-cutting hand, and keep that hand on the ruler until you've completed the cut. Keep fingers well back on the ruler and away from the blade to avoid accidents. ❏

Cutting with an art knife and ruler on a cutting mat.

Folding Tools

Folding is an important part of paper crafting, especially when making greeting cards. Learning to fold paper correctly is important for professional-looking results. Folding is a simple technique, and clean, crisp folds give your projects strength and a sculptured look. The folds catch the light, and the shadows add to the depth of the design. The best known technique for folding paper is the accordion fold – paper is folded back and forth, somewhat like the bellows of the musical instrument. More complicated origami folds can produce interesting effects.

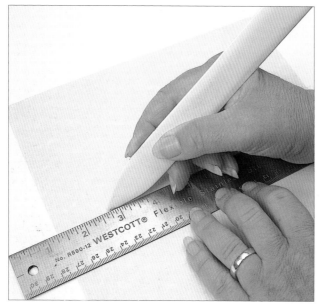

1. Score.

Bone Folder

A bone folder, which is formed from bone, is used to fold sharp creases, score fold lines, and help smooth and burnish papers. The bone does not bruise or scratch papers as plastic folders tend to do. An 8" bone folder with a pointed end is convenient for general work.

How to:
1. If the paper is translucent, you can place it directly on the cutting mat and follow the grid lines for straight folds. Or mark the fold lines using pencil.
2. Place a ruler on top of paper along the straight grid lines of mat or pencil mark.
3. For each fold, draw the bone folder along the ruler edge towards you, pressing down to score a fold line.
4. Fold along this scored line.
5. Use the bone folder to firmly reinforce each fold by pressing the fold down sharply. ❏

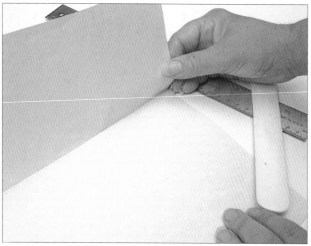

2. Fold.

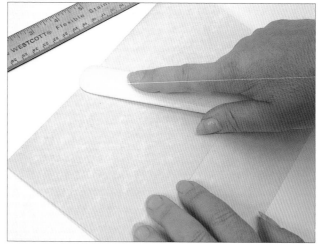

3. Press.

party time

Collage

A collage is a design or a picture created by arranging and adhering flat elements (decorative papers, ephemera, found paper items, or cloth) to a flat surface. Its name is derived from the French word *coller,* meaning "to paste." The process is widely used by artists from Pablo Picasso to Romare Bearden and is a familiar technique in contemporary art.

Many of us have childhood memories of creating collages for school or summer camp projects. Tearing and cutting words, photographs, and illustrations from magazine pages and gluing them to illustrate a theme is a familiar process.

Collages can be characterized as artistic combinations of everyday materials and objects. I like to think that a collage tells a story about an event, an emotion, or a color. Many elements in art collages come from "found" materials, such as images from magazines and newspapers, wallpaper designs, and paper ephemera items such as ticket stubs, labels, stamps and bills, to name a few. Many scrapbook pages, handmade cards, and artist trading cards fit under the collage designation.

The most important thing to remember about collage is that there are no rules! You don't need to be an artist to create a collage – but you do need to be proficient at simple techniques such as cutting, tearing, and gluing.

In this section, I share some simple hints and ideas to help take the mystery out of making collages. Lose those notions about perfection and measuring – be creative and unpredictable! Let collage free you and allow your inner artist to emerge. You will be pleasantly surprised at how your other paper crafting projects will improve!

Collage Glossary

Here are some techniques and definitions that are associated with the art of collage.

Assemblage – A collage with added three-dimensional objects. Examples of objects used include ribbons, charms, coins, buttons, and beads – collectively referred to as "embellishments." An assemblage with bulky embellishments is also called a **relief sculpture**.

Altered Art – A collage on a base that is altered with papers and embellishments. The base often altered is a book, both inside (on the pages) and outside (on the cover). Altered art takes collage to an exuberant creative space where almost everything can be used.

ATCs (Artist Trading Cards) – Miniature works of art on 2-1/2" x 3-1/2" pieces of card stock, traded in person or by mail. Never sold, they showcase all types of art techniques, including collage.

Beeswax Collage – A relatively new collage technique that uses melted beeswax as the "glue" for attaching collage elements, including embellishments, to a rigid surface.

Decoupage – A type of collage; a craft that uses cutout images adhered to a surface. The technique of decorating surfaces by adhering cutouts (usually paper), then coating the surface with one or more coats of a transparent or translucent finish such as decoupage medium or, more traditionally, lacquer or varnish.

Mixed Media – An art object that incorporates more than one medium – for example, a beeswax collage with papers, feathers, charms, and ribbons.

Montage – A collage that incorporates photographs.

Nature Collage – A collage made up of items collected from nature, such as pressed flowers or leaves and handmade papers.

Photomontage – A collage made entirely from photographs or parts of photographs.

Tissue Collage – A collage made of layers of tissue paper that create a design. Tissue collage can be combined with other collage and decoupage techniques.

Basic Supplies for Collage

Pictured above: 1)Glue stick; 2)Glue dots; 3)Decoupage medium and Brush; 4) Craft glue; 5) Scissors; 6) Decorative edge scissors; 7) Paper trimmer; 8) Art knife; 9) Cutting mat; 10) Bone folder; 11) Ruler; 12) Deckle edge ruler

Bases

The base is the surface on which you create your collage. It can be anything from a card blank to the cover of a journal. Bases used for the collage projects in this book include card blanks, purses, trays, coasters, papier mache boxes and letters, canvases, lampshades, and blank journals.

Adhesives for Collages

The adhesive or glue you use to attach the collage elements is determined by the base you are using and your chosen college elements. Here are some guidelines:

Glue stick: For paper bases, such as card blanks or journal covers, a glue stick works well. When working with a glue stick, use a gluing sheet (pieces of wax paper, deli sheets, or pages from an old phone book) to keep the front of your images free of excess glue.

Glue dots: Glue dots raise the paper image or embellishment off the surface and give a multi-layered effect to the collage. Glue dots are available in a variety of sizes from 1/8" to 1/2" in both circles and squares. Some glue dots are pieces of foam with adhesive on both sides; others are dimensional clear dots of glue on a protective paper roll.

Decoupage medium: On wood or canvas bases, use decoupage medium ("podge"-type mediums or thin-bodied white glue) to glue paper items to prepared surfaces. Use a 1/2" to 1" flat brush to apply the medium to the back of the paper. Podge-type mediums come in a variety of finishes, including gloss, satin, or matte, plus sepia-toned and pearl.

Craft glue: Thick, tacky white craft glue is used to apply heavier embellishments – it creates a much stronger bond than a hot glue gun. **Specialty craft glues**, such as jewelry glue and wood glue, work well on specific projects (e.g., use jewelry glue to attach embellishments to a metal surface). Craft glues are white when wet and dry crystal clear.

Thin-Bodied White Glue: Thin-bodied white glue contains latex and can be used to seal paper pieces before applying a polymer resin coating. It goes on white, dries crystal clear, and prevents the resin from bleeding onto the print and leaving a dark spot. For sealing, two thin coats are better than one heavy coat. Make sure the first coat is dry before brushing on a second coat, and be sure the second coat is totally dry and clear before applying the polymer coating. (If the glue is just a little bit damp, it will turn white under the coating and ruin the design.) **Do not** substitute a decoupage medium for the seal coat – most do not contain enough latex to seal the paper properly.

Basic Tools

These are the basic tools you need for creating collages:

Scissors, for cutting. A basic pair of straight edge scissors works well; decorative edge scissors give a variety of different edges to your design.

Paper Trimmer, for cutting squares, rectangles, and borders from decorative papers for abstract collages. I prefer the slide type of paper trimmer, which is readily available at crafts and art supply stores.

Art Knife (Craft Knife) with a #11 blade and a self-healing cutting mat are used to cut papers that cannot go through a paper trimmer, such as fine tissues or heavily textured handmade paper. The art knife is also used for cutting out the inside areas of images of decoupage prints.

Bone Folder, for pressing down paper pieces when adhering them to a surface. Use a bone folder for pressing folds and for removing wrinkles and creases.

Ruler, for tearing. A ruler is rarely used when creating a collage, but the straight edge is handy as a guide for tearing. A metal ruler with a cork backing is best. Rulers with decorative edges (e.g., deckle) are available for creating decorative torn edges.

Supplies for Distressing & Antiquing

You can use a variety of techniques to alter paper pieces to make them more interesting. Some of my favorites include:

Walnut ink, which can be brushed, sprayed, spattered, and stippled onto paper.
Strong solutions of tea or coffee, which can be used to soak papers for an aged look. The solution can also be brushed or spattered.
Fine sandpaper (300 grit), to lightly sand and distress the paper pieces.
Metallic paste wax can add soft metallic highlights.
    Use **petroleum jelly** as a resist for painted or distressed effects on collages.

Paper Images

Paper images come from a variety of sources. All types of printed paper images can be used – thin or thick, glossy or dull, smooth or textured, plain or patterned, colored or black and white. Handmade papers, decoupage paper, colored tissue, photographs, magazines, scrapbook papers, paper napkins, greeting cards, and wallpaper are all excellent sources for images.

Ephemera

Collage artists especially prize ephemera – the pieces of paper from everyday life, such as handwritten letters, pages from old books, old documents, and items such as tickets, labels, and certificates. You can find old ephemera in second-hand or antique stores, or raid your attic for old letters, postcards, and family records. TIP: Rather than use a precious or one-of-a-kind item or image to make your collage, color photocopy or scan and print it. **Always** copy valuable pieces rather than using originals in your projects.

You can also find ephemera re-printed on scrapbook paper or in books of one-sided pages ready to cut and use. (Find them at crafts and scrapbooking stores.)

Decorative Papers

Decorative papers come in a huge assortment of colors, designs, and textures. In one walk through the aisles of a scrapbooking, crafts, or art supply store, you will discover many papers to inspire you. Different types of decorative papers can be used for collages, from thin tissue papers, wrapping paper, and handmade papers to heavier card stock, memory papers, and art prints.

Decorative Elements

Stickers offer a huge variety of instant motifs that you simply peel and stick on your composition. I especially like using the "orphan" letters from sticker alphabets (ones left over from other projects). Mixing and matching the different letters can enhance a collage design. Look also for fine art stickers, vintage labels, and quotes printed on vellum. TIP: When you're planning your collage, roughly cut out the sticker, leaving the backing paper in place, until you are ready to affix it to the design.

continued on page 20

Pictured at right: A color-photocopied sheet is surrounded with various examples of ephemera and flat objects that can be scanned or photocopied. On top of the photocopied sheet are two artist trading collage cards created with the images.

Image Collections

Copyright infringement – the use of copyrighted material without permission – is a growing concern for collage artists because collages often incorporate elements of other works. Copyright laws can be confusing and guidelines for using copyrighted material are fraught with myth and misinformation.

Fortunately, there are sources of images that collage artists can use without fear of infringing others' rights. Scrapbooking, rubber stamp, and crafts stores sell paper image collections intended for collage work, and some publishers specialize in providing ready-to-use color and black-and-white images. Guidelines for use are set forth in the book (e.g., 10 images per book per collage).

Decoupage Papers

Decoupage papers offer endless design possibilities for collages. Lightweight, tissue-like decoupage papers are especially wonderful for layering and for beeswax collage.

Embellishments

Found items from around your house that can be used on collages include coins, corks, keys, and buttons. Raid your sewing room for scraps of fabric, ribbons, cords, and lace to add texture and interest to your designs.

Natural materials include shells, pine cones, pebbles, dried flowers, feathers, dried leaves, skeleton leaves, coral sand, and natural papers.

Decorative embellishments from craft and paper crafting stores include charms, silk flowers, clock parts, beads, tags, charms, eyelets, stickers, and metal and chipboard letters.

Pictured at right – Paper Images for Collages: 1) Decorative papers with matching stickers and vellum sayings; 2) Handmade papers; 3) Decoupage papers; 4) Collage image collections; 5) Vintage image booklets; 6) Photographs

tip: CREATING A STORAGE SYSTEM

When you have collected papers and items for your collage, you will need a system for storage and easy access. You can sort the collage materials by color, by theme, or by type of material. A variety of sophisticated storage systems are available, from containers for very small collections to larger bins.

I like to store my bits and pieces in zipper-top plastic bags, which I place in large plastic containers. This enables me to see all the materials without having them cluttered all together.

Designing your Collage

When creating a collage, there are no rules or limits. This very creative
art form offers the freedom to create with just about anything
and the opportunity to play!
But how to begin? What items work best? How do you know when your
collage is finished? These and other questions are answered on the following
pages, along with helpful hints and information on collage techniques.

Basic Steps for Starting a Collage

1. **Start small.** Begin with a small project, such as a greeting card.

2. **Choose a theme.** It can be anything! (a color, a mood, an emotion, an event, or a place, a person, or a thing) It can be as simple as "blue" or more complicated, such as "travel to Paris." It can be an abstract composition of colors and shapes, or a realistic composition with images of a subject or concept.

3. **Gather your materials.** Think of images, colors, photographs, textures, and ephemera that relate to your chosen theme and gather materials. Use quotes, words, or letters to help communicate the theme.

4. **Choose a focal point.** A focal point helps direct the eye; it can be a photo, a larger or contrasting image, a word, or a quotation. Think about framing this piece with a piece of contrasting paper behind it or edging the piece with a colored, inked edge.

5. **Plan the layout.** Lay out the pieces without gluing them. Here are some guidelines.
   • Start by placing the background pieces and largest pieces.
   • Cluster embellishments or small paper images in groups with an odd number of pieces (one, three, or five).
   • Vertical and horizontal lines are quiet; diagonal lines bring movement.
   • Use a variety of effects – rip some paper edges, cut others.
   • Repeating a motif, color, shape, or texture in your composition brings everything together. Variety is good, but repetition brings rhythm and pattern to a collage.
   • Squint at the composition to see if you achieved a balance with color tones.
   • Allow yourself to be impulsive.

6. **Re-evaluate.** When you think you are finished, step away for a while, then come back and re-evaluate the composition.
   Turn it upside down or sideways for a different perspective. Introduce a new element for contrast. Trust your instincts. Decide what looks good to you. Don't start gluing until you are happy with the arrangement.

Pictured at right: A collection of materials related by theme and color.

Preparing Paper Images

There are a variety of ways to treat paper images for use in collage. Play and experiment – try folding, coloring with chalks or stamping inks, scratching, piercing, weaving, or stitching. Here are a few ways to make your paper images more interesting:

Cutting

1. Trim away excess paper from around the motif.
2. Using an art knife, work on a cutting mat to cut out inside areas before cutting around the outer edge.
3. Use small, sharp, pointed scissors to cut out the design, holding the scissors at a 45-degree angle to cut the paper with a tiny beveled edge. (This will help the motif to rest snugly against the surface.) Move the paper, not the scissors as you cut.

Tearing

- Torn paper pieces without white edges will blend into the composition. To tear a piece of paper without a white edge, rip away from you.
- White edges on torn paper pieces will frame the torn piece and make it stand out. To tear a piece of paper with a white edge, rip towards you.
- To tear a straight edge, place a ruler on the paper. Use a brush to "paint" a line of clean water along the ruler. Position the ruler on the water line and tear carefully.
- You can also use a water line to tear shapes and wavy lines from paper.

Pictured above – Materials for distressing paper and examples: 1) Walnut ink, 2) Tea, 3) Coffee, 4) Sandpaper, 5) Samples of papers.

Crumpling

Here's how to create fine creases over an entire piece of paper. This technique looks especially nice when stained with tea or coffee for an antique look.
1. Carefully crumple the paper, un-crumple, then crumple and un-crumple again.
2. Smooth the paper on a flat surface.

Sanding

- To distress, use 300-grit sandpaper to lightly sand the surface of a paper piece just a little or lots.
- To create a sanded design on the paper, place the paper on a texture plate, then sand. You will pick up the texture on the front of the paper.
- Sand along the edge of a surface so paper will fit the edge of a base.

Pictured at left: Sanding the edge of a paper so it fits perfectly on a base.

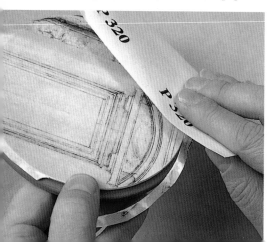

Antiquing Paper

Tea, coffee, walnut ink, and metallic wax are great for antiquing papers.

- For a **tea solution**, place 5 tea bags in 1/2 cup of boiling water and brew until cool. (Depending on the type of tea, you will get a wide range of tones.) For a **coffee solution**, place 2 tablespoons instant coffee in 1/2 cup boiling water, stir, and let cool. Place the paper you want to antique on wax paper. Use the solutions full strength or diluted to brush or spatter the paper. Do not disturb until completely dry.

- For a **mottled effect**, sprinkle coffee grinds or brewed tea leaves on the wet surface. Simply brush off the dried bits when the paper is dry.
- **Walnut ink** is available as crystals or a liquid. I prefer the pre-mixed liquid walnut ink that comes in handy spray bottles. You can also brush or spatter liquid walnut ink.
- **Metallic paste wax** works especially well on beeswax collages – simply apply it with your finger, let dry, and buff. You can also add a soft metallic gleam to decoupage papers with metallic wax.

Gluing Images

Arrange your composition, moving the pieces around before gluing. When you are happy with the arrangement, then start to permanently adhere them to the surface. Use the recommended glue for the best results. See "Adhesives for Collages" in the Basic Materials section for details.

For medium-weight paper pieces:

1. Place freezer paper or wax paper on your work surface to protect it.
2. Lightly coat the back of the image with decoupage medium or thin-bodied glue. (Too much glue will cause excessive wrinkling that cannot be corrected.) Work from the center of the paper piece to the outside, making sure you have glue on all the edges and that there is an even coating of glue on the paper.
3. Lift the paper piece and place it on the surface.
4. Use your fingers to carefully smooth the image, then use your fingers or a bone folder to remove wrinkles and bubbles. Larger pieces are the most likely to have bubbles and wrinkles – work fast. Let the glue dry before proceeding.

For thinner papers, such as tissue or fine handmade paper:

1. Brush decoupage medium on the surface.
2. Position and attach the paper piece.
3. Immediately brush medium over the paper to adhere it and smooth out any wrinkles.

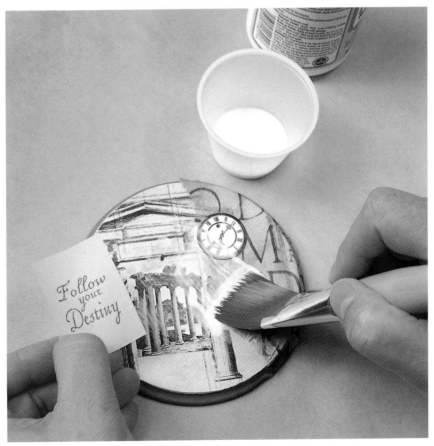

Using decoupage medium to adhere paper elements.

Continued on next page

Gluing Images, continued

Overlapping Papers

Create interesting backgrounds by layering papers to build up textures. For best results, use thinner papers (thin handmade papers, the top printed layer of paper napkins, tissue papers). Heavier papers can be layered for heavier textured effects.

Creating a Resist

Use petroleum jelly as a resist to create vintage effects on collages.

1. When you have glued your collage, apply two to three coats of acrylic varnish. Let dry.
2. Rub a thin coat of petroleum jelly over the collage.
3. Paint with one coat of acrylic paint. Let dry.
4. Use a soft cloth to rub off the paint and create the antique effect. The paint will peel off where the petroleum jelly was applied.

Rubbing off paint applied over a petroleum jelly resist to reveal the collage.

Protecting the Finished Collage

Properly protected, your finished work will last and you will be able to enjoy it for years. Options include acrylic varnish, dimensional varnish, and two-part polymer coating.

Acrylic Varnish

Acrylic varnishes come in gloss, satin, and matte sheens, as well as sepia-tints, metallics, pearl tones, and iridescents for special effects. On painted surfaces, apply two or three coats of acrylic varnish to protect and beautify. Here's how:

1. Roll the varnish container instead of shaking it to minimize the appearance of bubbles on your finished piece.
2. Pour the varnish into a small disposable bowl (this prevents the large container from being contaminated as you work).
3. Use a large, soft brush to apply the varnish to the surface in slow, thin coats. Let each coat dry thoroughly before adding another layer. The more thin coats you apply, the tougher the surface will be.

To care for a varnished surface, simply wipe with a damp cloth. **For tough stains or marks,** gently sand with a very fine grit sandpaper until the mark is gone. Re-varnish the piece with at least two coats.

Dimensional Varnish

Dimensional varnish dries clear and adds a slight dimension. Available in clear, sepia, and antique hues, it creates a shiny, dimensional paper piece without using a polymer coating. Dimensional varnish comes in a bottle with a narrow opening that allows you to squeeze varnish onto individual paper pieces. Here's how to use it:

1. After the paper pieces are decoupaged to the surface, topcoat the surface with decoupage medium. Let dry.
2. Squeeze dimensional varnish on the paper pieces one at a time, being careful not to let the varnish flow off the edge. TIP: Outline each piece, then fill in the center area. Leave undisturbed until dry.

Polymer Coating

A polymer coating is a liquid plastic coating that can be poured on a variety of surfaces. When dry and cured, it provides a thick, permanent, waterproof, high-gloss surface. The coating comes in two parts, a resin and a hardener. When equal amounts of the two parts are mixed together, they react chemically to form the plastic coating. The coating is chemically inert once it has cured and, when cured, can be drilled or sanded.

You will experience the best results when you work in a dust-free room with a temperature of 75 to 80 degrees F. and humidity under 50 percent.

GENERAL SUPPLIES for Polymer Coating
Two part pour-on polymer coating
Plastic mixing cups with accurate measurement marks
   (They're sold alongside the coating.)
Wooden stir stick (craft stick)
Disposable glue brush
Freezer paper *or* wax paper
Clear cellophane tape
Sandpaper
Thin-bodied white glue

BASIC STEPS for Applying a Polymer Coating

1. **Seal the project.** Seal the paper with two thin coats of white glue before coating. If the paper is not sealed properly, the resin will seep and create a dark mark. Let the glue seal coat dry completely dry before proceeding.

2. **Prepare the project surface.** The polymer coating will drip off the sides of the project, so to prevent drips forming on the bottom, protect the underside by covering the bottom edges with clear cellophane tape. Apply tape to the underside edge of the item and press the tape firmly. If there's any hardware you don't want covered with the coating, remove it.

3. **Prepare your work area.** Your work surface must be clean, level, and protected well with wax paper or freezer paper. The item you are covering should be lifted off the work surface about 2" to allow the resin to drip freely off the sides. **(Photo 1)** (I use small disposable plastic cups for this. For smaller pieces, such as jewelry, use wooden toothpicks stuck into pieces of plastic foam to elevate them.)

4. **Measure.** When the glue seal coats have dried completely clear, you are now ready to mix the polymer coating. The polymer coating comes in two parts, the resin and the hardener. If you're working in a cold area, warm the resin by placing the bottles in a bowl of warm (not hot) tap water. Place the mixing container on a level surface and put one part resin and one part hardener (exact amounts by volume) into the container. Measure exactly – do not guess – or your coating will be soft and sticky. Mix only as much as you can use at one time – leftover coating cannot be saved. On average, four ounces of mixed coating covers one square foot. Mix a minimum of two ounces.

5. **Mix** the resin and hardener vigorously with a wooden stir stick until thoroughly blended – a full two minutes. The importance of thorough mixing cannot be over-emphasized, as poor mixing can result in a soft finish. Scraping the sides and bottom of the container continually while mixing is a must. Do not be concerned if bubbles get whipped into the mixture. They are a sign that you are mixing well, and they can be removed after the coating is poured.

6. **Pour** right away, do not wait. Pour the coating over the surface of your item in a circular pattern, starting close to the edge and working towards the center. **(Photo 2)** This allows the resin to level out. Help spread where necessary with a disposable glue brush, but don't spread the coating too thin or the surface will be wavy. You have approximately 25 minutes to

continued on next page

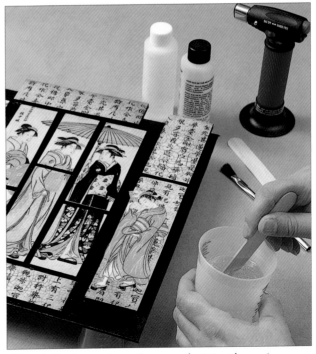

Photo 1. Setting up the work area and mixing the coating.

Polymer Coating, continued

work before the coating starts to set up. On paper mosaics, use the brush to remove excess coating from the "grout" lines (the spaces between the paper pieces). (**Photo 3**)

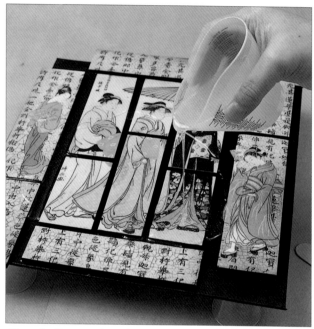

Photo 2 . Pouring the polymer coating over the surface.

7. **De-Gas.** Within 10 minutes of pouring, air bubbles created while mixing will rise to the surface and begin to break. Gently exhale (but don't blow) across the surface – the carbon dioxide in your breath will break the bubbles. On large surfaces, use a small propane torch to remove air bubbles. Hold the torch three to four inches from the surface. (**Photo 4**) **The resin contains no flammable solvents, and gases from a propane flame are rich in carbon dioxide. (It is the carbon dioxide – not the heat of the torch – that removes the bubbles.)**

8. Remove drips. Wait 30 minutes, then wipe away any drips from the bottom of the project with a glue brush. Wait 30 minutes more and repeat. After the coating has cured, remove any tape from the bottom edge of your item, and the drips will pop off. TIP: If you didn't use tape, sand off unwanted drips of cured coating. A circular sanding attachment on a hand drill works well.

9. **Allow to cure.** Allow the coated item to cure in a warm, dust-free room that is closed to pets and children for a full 72 hours for a hard and permanent finish before using or displaying. Discard the mixing cup, the stir stick, and the brush.

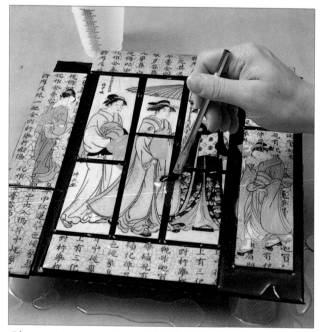

Photo 3. Using a brush to remove excess coating from the "grout" lines on a paper mosaic.

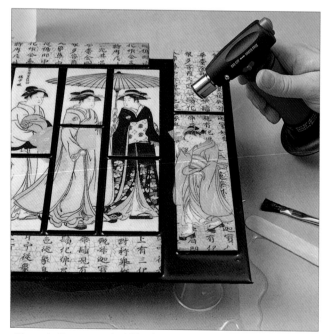

Photo 4. De-gassing bubbles from the surface with a propane torch.

Tissue Paper Collage

Brightly colored tissue paper can be layered to create interesting effects. Readily available and inexpensive, tissue paper can be used to create many collage projects. The simple projects in this section show the versatility of tissue paper.

Color Transfer with Tissue Paper

This technique produces a blended colored paper. It's inexpensive and requires no paints or inks – the color comes from the colored tissue paper. (You want the type labeled "bleeding tissue.") The white card paper you place underneath the tissue will be beautifully colored with interesting patterns and can be used for card making or other paper projects.

SUPPLIES

Spray bottle filled with clean water, for misting
Freezer paper *or* wax paper, to protect your work surface
Several sheets of colored tissue paper
White card stock

INSTRUCTIONS

1. Choose a work space where you can leave the paper undisturbed for the first stage of drying. Cover your work area with freezer paper or wax paper.
2. Cut the tissue paper slightly smaller than the white card stock. Place the white card stock on your work surface and spray lightly with water.
3. Place a piece of colored tissue on top. Mist lightly with water.
4. Repeat with different colors of tissue, spraying with water each time until you have four to six sheets on top of each other. Let the pile sit to allow the dyes from the tissue sheets to mix and mingle. NOTE: If you're disappointed with how the tissue paper looks when it's wet, don't give up! Let it dry completely before judging your success. The subtle patterns and colors aren't revealed until the paper is completely dry.
5. When the sheets are just damp – nearly dry – lift off the individual sheets of tissue and lay flat until completely dry. ❑

Tissue paper is layered on a work surface and misted with water.

Dry sheets of tissue paper after the color transfer technique.

Seaside Scenes
cards

These seaside-themed cards use up all those miscellaneous stickers and orphan paper scraps you've been saving. The simple block shapes of the main paper images and the transparent stickers keep the compositions from looking too busy.

SUPPLIES

Base:

4 cream or light green card blanks, 4-1/4" x 5-1/4" (folded size)

4 matching envelopes

Papers:

White lightweight card, 8-1/2" x 11"

Japanese papers – Teals, greens

Seaside images

Sandpaper

Silver metallic paper

Stickers

Vellum stickers with sayings

Vellum shell stickers

Embellishments:

Shell novelty buttons, shanks removed

Tools & Other Supplies:

Scissors

Glue stick

White craft glue

INSTRUCTIONS

1. Tear the Japanese papers into 1" wide strips.
2. Using a glue stick, glue the strips to the white card paper, overlapping them, to make the backgrounds for the cards.
3. Cut four 4" x 5" panels from the background paper (you can get four panels per sheet).
4. Glue the panels to the fronts of the cards.
5. Trim four seaside images. Glue each one to a panel of either sandpaper or silver paper to create the look of a frame.
6. Glue the framed image panels to the cards.
7. Add vellum shell stickers and a saying sticker to each card.
8. Use white craft glue to adhere the button embellishments. ❑

make a SPLASH.

I love the sea as I do my own soul
HEINRICH HEINE

THE Voice OF THE Sea SPEAKS TO THE Soul
KATE CHOPIN

the Secret of the Sea

A Collage on the Wild Side
wooden purse

The theme of this collage is "wild" – perfect for a fun purse design.
To make the collage, I used a combination of
decoupage papers and napkins with different animal prints.

SUPPLIES

Base:
D-shaped wooden purse,
  10" x 7-1/2" x 3"
Bamboo handle
Purse clamps

Papers:
Wild animal images from paper
  napkins
Newspaper clippings (type or animal
  engravings)
Animal print decoupage paper
Animal print suede paper

Embellishments:
2 bottle caps
2 round stickers, 1"
Tiny plastic animals
Lowercase chipboard letters to spell
  "wild," 2-1/2" or 3" tall
Acrylic paints – Black, green
Dimensional paint – Clear
Beads that match the theme
Zebra charm
Waxed linen cord
Ribbons that match the theme,
  10" pieces

Tools & Other Supplies:
Painting sponge
Decoupage medium, matte sheen
Brush
Rubber mallet
Optional: Tea bags

INSTRUCTIONS

1. Remove all the hardware from the purse and set aside.
2. Tear the animal print papers into strips 2" to 3" wide. (You need enough strips to cover the top and sides of the front and back of the purse.)
3. Using decoupage medium, paste the animal print papers across surface in an overlapping, diagonal pattern. Let dry.
4. Cover the inside edges of the purse with paper strips.
5. *Option:* Antique the newspaper clippings and wild animal images with a tea solution to give them an aged appearance. Let dry.
6. On the front of the purse, create a collage of newspaper clippings and wild animal images.
7. Sponge the acrylic paints on the chipboard letters, creating a mottled black and green effect. Let dry.
8. Coat the letters with a layer of clear dimensional paint. Let dry.
9. Flatten the bottle caps by hammering with a rubber mallet.
10. Put the round stickers in the centers of the caps. *Option:* Cut 1" circles from matching decorative paper and glue to the centers of the caps.
11. Coat the centers of the caps with a layer of clear dimensional paint. Let dry.
12. Glue the bottle caps and plastic animals to the purse front, using white craft glue.
13. Re-attach the hardware to the purse. Add the bamboo handle.
14. Make a tassel by threading a variety of beads on the waxed linen thread. Tie to the handle. Fold the ribbons in half and tie with a piece of linen thread to the handle. Glue the charm to the top of the tassel. ❑

Architectural Images
coasters

These coasters are an example of how to use a color and a theme to create a collage.
Coated with a polymer resin coating, they are washable, practical works of art.

SUPPLIES

Base:
4 round wooden coasters, 4-1/2"

Papers:
Architecture theme wrapping paper
  or architectural drawing
Torn piece of ocher paper napkin
Images of buildings
Vellum quotes
Round stickers

Tools & Other Supplies:
Scissors
Thin white glue
Polymer coating supplies (See the
  beginning of this section for a
  list.)
Cork buttons
Acrylic paint – Ocher
Paint brush
Sandpaper

INSTRUCTIONS

1. Basecoat the coasters with ocher acrylic paint. Let dry.
2. Cut a piece of architecture theme paper for each coaster that is 1/2" larger than the size of the coaster.
3. Glue the paper pieces to the tops of the coasters with white glue. Smooth out wrinkles or creases. Let dry completely.
4. Sand the edges of the paper to trim it exactly to the edges of the coasters.
5. Separate the plies of the paper napkin. Tear the top layer into 2" to 3" pieces. Glue a piece to each coaster, overlapping the edges.
6. Trim the building images into squares or rectangles. Glue one to each coaster, placing the pieces slightly off center.
7. Tear the vellum quotes and glue to the coasters. The vellum will wrinkle when glue is applied but will dry flat.
8. Add the round stickers.
9. Seal the finished collages with two thin coats of white glue. Let dry completely.
10. Apply the polymer coating. See "Basic Steps for Applying a Polymer Coating" for instructions.
11. When fully cured, add cork buttons to the bottoms. ❑

tip: If you find a paper with suitable motifs but you don't like the color, photocopy the paper in black and white or in a brown or sepia monotone using a color copier.

Memories Monogram
wall piece

This assemblage collage uses large papier mache letters and small stretched canvases as its base. I chose French images in coordinating colors for the collage and used the petroleum jelly resist technique to outline the letters and give an antique appearance.

SUPPLIES

Base:
3 papier mache letters, 8" tall
2 stretched canvases, 5" square

Papers:
Images and stickers to match your theme

Embellishments:
Label holder
Keys and keyhole charms
Jewelry findings
Small objects to fit your theme (e.g., Eiffel Tower)
Buttons
Ribbon
Metal corner charms

Tools & Other Supplies:
Acrylic paints – Gray-green, cream
White craft glue
Decoupage medium
Petroleum jelly
Large rubber bands
Soft cloth
Hanger(s)

INSTRUCTIONS

1. Experiment with your letters and canvases to make a pleasing arrangement.
2. Basecoat the letters with gray-green acrylic paint. Let dry.
3. Cover the canvases and letters with collage pieces, using decoupage medium. Let dry.
4. Seal all the pieces with two coats of decoupage medium. Let dry.
5. Glue letters and canvases together, arranging them as before, using craft glue. Hold the pieces together while they dry with large rubber bands for a strong bond.
6. Rub a thin coat of petroleum jelly over the fronts of the letters.
7. Paint the letters with one coat of cream acrylic paint. Let dry.
8. When the paint is dry, rub off the paint from the letters with a soft cloth to create the antique effect.
9. Glue the label holder and other embellishments to the collage with white craft glue. Let dry.
10. Attach the hanger(s) to the back. Take into account the balance of the finished piece to determine where to place the hanger(s) so the arrangement will hang properly. ❏

Asian Accents
journal cover

An Asian theme that includes images of geishas and ephemera in shades of purple and lilac was used for this collage on the front of a blank journal. The design uses layers of very sheer Japanese paper to create a soft, veiled effect on some of the images.

SUPPLIES

Base:

Blank journal with cream paper cover, 8" square, bound with cord

Papers:

Japanese papers in shades of purple and lilac

Sheer Japanese paper

Images of Japanese geishas

Asian money and travel stickers

Embellishments:

Resin tile stickers, 3/8" square

8 copper corner brads

14 purple paper flowers, 3/4"

3 pieces pink paper cord, each 8" long

20" purple variegated sheer ribbon

Purple cord with tassel

Thin metallic paper cords

Tools & Other Supplies:

Glue stick

Bone folder

Glue dots, foam backed

INSTRUCTIONS

1. Remove the existing binding cord. Replace with variegated ribbon.
2. Start the collage by arranging the large purple paper panels, the main image, and the money stickers. When you are happy with the arrangement, use a glue stick to adhere the purple paper panels.
3. Add the secondary images, travel stickers, and money stickers. Place the stickers so they overlap the spine and wrap around the edges of the cover.
4. Place the metallic paper cords diagonally on the cover and glue in place.
5. Glue the trimmed main image to a lilac paper panel with a glue stick.
6. Add corner brads to the framed image, and place it on the journal with glue dots over the metallic paper cord pieces.
7. Place sheer paper panels over some of the images, using a glue stick.
8. Arrange and glue the paper flowers in place with glue dots. Do not place them over the fold of the spine.
9. Add the tassel.
10. Use the same images and materials to decorate the inside of the journal. ❏

Two for a Writer
wooden box & journal

The box is stamped with texture rubber stamps and thermal embossed to create an interesting surface for the collage. Stamped images and images from decorative papers are used to cover the box and journal. Stamping and embossing with the same colors creates a coordinated pair.

SUPPLIES

Base:

Kraft paper blank journal, 5" x 7"

Wooden box with sliding top, 7-1/4" x 10-1/2"

Papers:

Renaissance images in shades of browns and muted colors

Bird-theme postage stamps

Old script images

Images of black and white lettering, pen nibs, and desk items

Beige card stock

Embellishments:

Copper dragonfly charms

Tools & Other Supplies:

Rubber stamps – Flourish, heart, textures

Pigment inkpad – Dark brown

Dark brown embossing powder

Embossing tool

Decoupage medium

Acrylic stain – Brown

Decorative scissors – Stamp edge

Soft cloth

Optional: Acrylic varnish

INSTRUCTIONS

Stain the Box:

Stain the box by brushing it with acrylic stain and immediately rubbing off the stain with a soft cloth. Let dry.

Stamp the Box:

1. Stamp an image on the box. Sprinkle the ink with embossing powder and tap off the excess.
2. Heat the stamped image with the embossing tool until the powder melts and turns shiny.
3. Repeat, stamping and embossing motifs over the top and sides of the box.

Prepare the Papers:

1. Stamp and emboss images on beige card stock. Cut out the images.
2. Cut out the Renaissance and black and white images.
3. Tear pieces of the script images.
4. Cut out the stamp images with decorative edge scissors.

Create the Collages:

1. Start by arranging the larger images, working on the top of the box, all the sides of the box, and the journal cover. Add smaller images until you are satisfied with the arrangement.
2. Glue all images to the surfaces with decoupage medium, being careful not to get any medium on the fronts of the images.
3. *Option:* Add an acrylic varnish topcoat. Let dry.
4. Add the copper charms with white craft glue. ❑

BASIC SUPPLIES

For each necklace:

Colored card stock

Metal bezel frames – rectangles

2 fold-over connector findings

2 jump rings

1 toggle clasp set

For the Gibson Girl Pendant:

Card stock – Blue, gray

Marbled paper

Paper scraps

Image for bezel – Lady in corset

Cherub charm

Black cord

2 pieces blue decorative fibers,
    each 24"

For the Girls Pendant:

Card stock – Dark green, plum

Papers scraps

Green corrugated paper scraps

Image for bezel – Young girls

Cherub charm

Black cord

2 pieces green decorative fibers,
    each 24"

For the Pig Pendant:

Card stock – Tan, terra cotta

Marbled paper

Papers scraps

Image for bezel – Drinking pig

Cherub charm

Black cord

2 pieces brown decorative fibers,
    24" each

For the polymer coating:

Thin-bodied white glue

Polymer coating supplies (See the
    beginning of this section for a
    list.)

Diamond Pendants
mini collages

These diamond-shaped pendants are examples of mini-collage.
All three use the same techniques but different images,
themes, and colors. For variation, consider using round,
triangular, or square shapes for the base.

BASIC INSTRUCTIONS

1. Cut the colored card stock into 2" x 3" diamond shapes.

2. Arrange the diamond shapes with a collage paper pieces cut from the paper scraps and metal frame until you are happy with the result.

3. Glue everything together.

4. Apply two coats of white glue. Let the first coat dry. Add the charm while the last coat of glue is still wet. Let dry completely, until clear.

5. Coat the pendant with polymer coating. See "Basic Steps for Applying a Polymer Coating" for instructions.

6. When cured, finish the necklace by laying out the black cord and decorative fibers. Thread the center of the bundle through the top of the metal frame and secure with a loop knot.

7. Using white glue, glue the ends of the cords into the connectors and fold over to hold tight.

8. Attach the toggle clasp pieces to the connectors using jump rings. ❑

BASIC SUPPLIES

These are the basic supplies you need to make this type of bracelet, no matter which style you choose to make.

Base:
Mat board – 3" x 8"

Paper:
Collage image – 2" x 7"
2 or 3 smaller, related images

Jewelry Supplies:
Beading wire – 20" per bracelet
Crimp beads – 4 per bracelet
Toggle clasp – 1 per bracelet
30 (approx.) crystal beads, 4mm
Seed beads
Charm and jump ring
Metallic paste

Tools & Other Supplies:
Crimping tool *or* jewelry pliers
Wire cutters
Thin-bodied white glue
Brush
Art knife, cutting mat and ruler
Polymer coating supplies (See the be-
   ginning of this section for a list.)
Acrylic craft paint (a color that coor-
   dinates with the main image)
Sandpaper
Drill and 1/16" drill bit

PROJECT SUPPLIES

For the Corset Bracelet:
• The mat board was cut into seven
   pieces, each 1-3/4" x 3/4".
• The 4mm beads are black crystal;
   the seed beads are green.
• The charm is a safety pin.
• The metallic paste is silver.

For the Menu Bracelet:
• The mat board was cut into seven
   pieces, each 2" x 3/4".
• The 4mm beads are amber crystal;
   the seed beads are gold.
• The charm is a spoon.
• The metallic paste is copper.

Pictures Tell a Story
linked bracelets

These stylish, fun-to-wear bracelets are examples
of mini-collage. The two designs are made using
the same techniques. These bracelets are about 7-1/2" long;
add or subtract segments to fit.

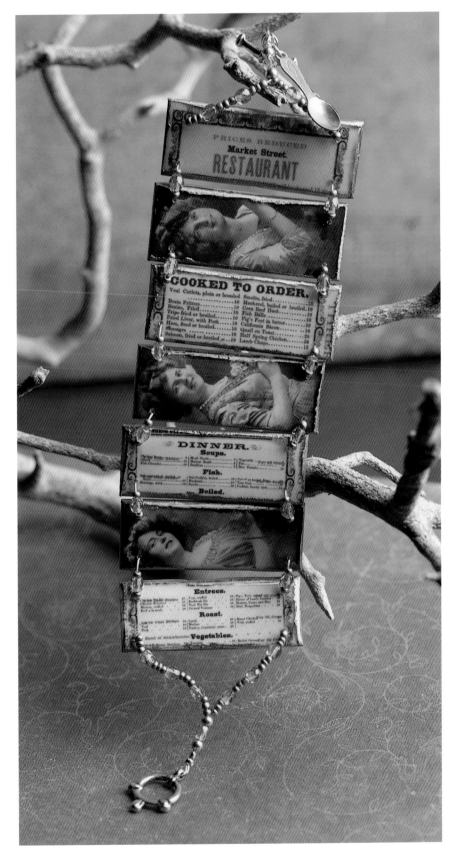

BASIC INSTRUCTIONS

Make the Collage Links:

1. Using thin-bodied white glue, glue the main image to the mat board.
2. Add additional paper images to the collage. Let dry.
3. Seal with two coats of the glue. Let dry completely.
4. Place the mat board on the cutting mat. Cut the image into seven rectangular pieces (each 3/4" x 1-1/2", 3/4" x 2", etc.). TIPS: Don't cut through an important element of the picture, such as a face. Cut a selection of images, then mix and match them as I did for the Menu Bracelet.

Coat & Paint:

1. Coat the mat board pieces with polymer coating. See "Basic Steps for Applying a Polymer Coating" for instructions.
2. When completely cured, remove any drips on the backs of the pieces by sanding.
3. Paint the backs of the pieces. Let dry.
4. Using metallic paste, add a metallic edge around each piece.

Start Beading:

1. Using a 1/16" bit, drill four holes in each piece. Use the photos as guides for placing the holes.
2. Thread the beading wire through the end of the round toggle piece with the center of the wire through the loop. Hold the ends of the beading wire together and thread on two crimp beads. Crimp to hold.
3. On both wires, add 1 seed bead, 1 crystal bead, and 1 seed bead.
4. Thread on one wire: 3 seeds, 1 crystal, 3 seeds, 1 crystal, 3 seeds, 1 crystal, and 3 seeds.
5. Repeat this sequence on the other wire.

Continued on next page

Pictures Tell a Story Linked Bracelets, continued

Add the Links:

1. Add the coated link pieces in order. Work on one side first, in this order: Thread the wire through the top hole of the first coated piece and up through the bottom of the next drilled hole. Thread on 1 seed bead, 1 crystal bead, and 1 seed bead. Thread into the next piece from the top. Repeat the sequence until you have all the links threaded on the wire with beads between each piece. Clamp to hold.
2. Repeat the sequence on the other side.

Finish:

1. Thread the following on one wire: 3 seeds, 1 crystal, 3 seeds, 1 crystal, and 3 seeds.
2. Repeat this sequence on the other wire.
3. On both wires, add 1 seed bead, 1 crystal bead, 1 seed bead, 2 crimp beads, and the rod toggle piece. TIP: Add extra seed or crystal beads before the toggle to enlarge the size of the bracelet.
4. Thread the wire back through the crimp beads and 3 seed beads. Adjust the wire and beads. Crimp the crimp beads to hold. Trim off the excess wire.
5. Add a charm on a jump ring as an accent. ❑

All About Me
photomontage purse

This metal box purse is decorated with a photomontage collage. Using black-and-white photos removes the color element from the collage design; cropping them into similar shapes makes this an easy project for beginners.

TIPS: Photocopying the photographs in black and white using a color copier yields best results. If you use photos printed on an inkjet printer, spray them with several coats of clear varnish to prevent the ink from bleeding. You can enlarge and reduce the images as you like.

SUPPLIES

Base:
Metal purse, 7-1/4" x 5" x 3"

Paper:
Photocopies *or* prints of photos

Embellishments:
Flower stickers in bright colors
6 different ribbon pieces, each 12", 1/4" to 1" wide – Pinks, greens, yellow
Flower novelty button

Tools & Other Supplies:
Paper trimmer
Decoupage medium, matte finish
Brush
Craft glue

INSTRUCTIONS

1. Crop photos to make square and rectangular pieces, using a paper trimmer.
2. Starting with the larger images, cover the front and back of the purse by gluing on the images with decoupage medium. Overlap the images and wrap them around the edges and onto the sides. Let dry.
3. Coat the finished photomontage with two coats of decoupage medium. Let dry.
4. Add the flower stickers to add bright bits of color to the arrangement.
5. Coat the photomontage and stickers with a final application of decoupage medium.
6. Add flower stickers to the sides of the purse. (These pieces don't need to be coated.)
7. Wrap the ribbon lengths around the purse handle to make a tassel. Tie the ribbons together at the top with a piece of thin ribbon. Glue on a novelty button. ❑

Seeds of Friendship
tea tray

This nature-inspired collage uses pressed flowers, mica sheets, seeds, and skeleton leaves as the decorative elements along with decoupage papers. It's created on a canvas board placed in a wooden frame. To protect the collage from spills, coat the canvas board with a polymer coating or top it with a piece of glass cut to size.

SUPPLIES

Base:
Canvas board, 11" x 14"

Collage Elements:
Tissue decoupage paper with script writing
Tissue decoupage paper with hydrangea blossoms
Scrapbook paper with stone tiles
Scrapbook stickers of tiled letters
Sayings stickers on clear backing
Pressed flowers
Skeleton leaves
Flower seeds
Mica tiles

Embellishments:
4 silver cabinet knobs (for feet)
2 pulls (for handles)
White tassels

Tools & Other Supplies:
100 grit sandpaper
Acrylic varnish, satin finish
Decoupage medium, matte finish
White frame, 12" x 15"
Glass to fit frame *or* polymer coating supplies (See the beginning of this section for a list.)
Scissors
Acrylic paint – Soft yellow
Brush

INSTRUCTIONS

Prepare:
1. Sand the white frame to distress. Wipe away dust.
2. Coat with satin varnish and set aside.
3. Basecoat the canvas board with the soft yellow acrylic paint. Let dry.

Create the Collage:
1. Glue the larger pieces of script decoupage paper and tissue paper to the painted board.
2. Add stone tiles cut from the scrapbook paper. Cut different sizes of tiles. See the project photo for placement ideas.
3. Cut hydrangea images from the decoupage paper. Glue to the collage.
4. Add images of individual blossoms. See "Making Your Own Flower Images for Collages."
5. Apply saying stickers to the small tiles on the collage.
6. Cut out the tile letters to spell SEEDS OF FRIENDSHIP. Glue them on the collage.
7. Using decoupage medium, glue the skeleton leaves and seeds.
8. Coat the entire collage with two coats of decoupage medium.
9. Place the mica tiles and glue in place with a heavy coat of decoupage medium. Weight them while drying to keep them flat.

Finish:
1. *Option:* Apply a polymer coating to the collage. See "Basic Steps for Applying a Polymer Coating" for instructions.
2. Attach the knobs to the bottom of the frame for feet.
3. Attach a pull at each end for handles. Wrap the tassel around one handle.
4. Place the canvas in the frame and secure. Use the glass if you didn't apply a polymer coating. ❏

MAKING YOUR OWN FLOWER IMAGES FOR COLLAGES

For easier handling and more lasting colors, I prefer to color photocopy fresh or pressed flowers to use in collages. Here's how:

1. Create master sheets for copying by arranging the blossoms on a piece of 8-1/2" x 11" paper.
   - You can place single blossoms on the sheet or group the blossoms in tiny arrangements.
   - Choose a variety of background colors or match them to a particular project. That way it's easy to trim around the blossoms by leaving a tiny border of paper. For this project, for example, I photocopied the blossoms on a soft yellow sheet of paper.

   - You can use fresh pressed or dried pressed blossoms. Use a tiny drop of glue to hold each flower in place.
   - Try to fill up the whole sheet for more economical copying.
2. Copy the pages and cut out the images.

   If you're using an inkjet copier, spray them with several coats of clear varnish to prevent the ink from bleeding. If you're using a toner copier, varnish isn't needed.

Tissue Paper Collage
gift containers

These containers are made from collages created from color-transferred tissue paper – both the color-transferred tissue papers and the card paper base are used. Using decoupage medium to glue the tissue paper pieces makes the paper containers very strong and durable. Each container uses a slightly different technique, illustrating different methods of tissue paper collage, and each is a different size. The Green Container is 7" x 5"; the Floral Container is 7" x 4"; the Blue Container is 6" x 3-1/2".

SUPPLIES

White card stock, 12" square
Scissors
Spray bottle
Decoupage medium
Brush
Double-sided tape

For the Green Container:
Green and blue bleeding tissue paper
3-D sticker
2 small silver clips
3 different ribbons, each 12" long –
   Brown and turquoise

For the Floral Container:
Pink, purple, blue, and green
   bleeding tissue paper
Clear resin word stickers
Small silver clip
3 different ribbons, each 12" long –
   Pink and turquoise

For the Blue Container:
Blue, teal, and purple bleeding tissue
   paper
Flower punches – Various sizes
Letter stickers
Small black clip
3 different ribbons, each 12" long –
   Blue and white

INSTRUCTIONS

Make the Green Tissue Paper Collage:

1. Using shades of blue and green bleeding tissue paper, make color-transferred tissue papers using the white card stock as a base. See the section on "Tissue Paper Collage" earlier in this book for instructions.

2. Cut squares and rectangles in a variety of sizes (1" to 3") pieces from the color transferred tissue.

3. Glue the tissue paper pieces to the now-colored white card using decoupage medium, overlapping the pieces as you go.

4. Coat the entire surface with decoupage medium. Let dry.

5. Cut the tissue paper collage to 7-1/2" x 11".

Make the Floral Collage:

1. From shades of pink, purple, blue and green bleeding tissue paper, cut out flower and circle shapes. TIP: Multiple layers (up to eight) can be cut at one time to make this an easy task.

Continued on next page

Tissue Paper Collage Gift Containers, continued

2. Following the instructions earlier in this book (see the section on "Tissue Paper Collage"), make color-transferred tissue papers by layering the flower shapes on the white card. You'll have flower shapes in mixed colors on the white paper and color transferred tissue shapes.

3. Use decoupage medium to glue the flower tissue pieces to the now-colored white card. Overlap the pieces as you go.

4. Coat the entire surface with decoupage medium. Let dry.

5. Cut the tissue paper collage to 7-1/2" x 8-1/2".

Make the Blue Collage:

1. Using shades of blue and green bleeding tissue paper, make color-transferred tissue papers using the white card stock as a base. See the section on "Tissue Paper Collage" earlier in this book for instructions.

2. From shades of blue, teal, and purple color-transferred tissue, punch out flower shapes with the punches. TIP: To successfully punch lightweight tissue, place three or four layers in the punch at one time.

3. Glue the punched flower tissue pieces to the now-colored white card, overlapping the pieces as you go.

4. Coat the entire surface with decoupage medium. Let dry.

5. Cut the tissue paper collage to 6-1/2" square.

Make the Container:

These are general instructions for making a Column Twist Container.

1. Form a cylinder with the tissue paper collage. Use the double-sided tape to adhere the sides.

2. Pinch one end of the cylinder and fold up a 1/2" tab.

3. Following the fold, trim the inner side of the folded tab to reduce the bulk. Use double-sided tape to adhere the tab to close the end.

4. Pinch the other end at right angles to the first end to create the container. Place the gift inside and hold closed with the clip.

5. Decorate the container with stickers. Loop the ribbons through one side of a clip. ❏

Tissue Paper Mosaics
lampshades

These lampshades show how tissue paper collage can enhance almost any surface. The spaces between the tissue paper "tiles" allow the light to shine through the shade, creating a striking look when the lamp is turned on. A color-coordinated beaded tassel is attached around the neck of the lamp base. You can use these shades on any type of lamp base, and you can make any size lampshade. Choose a base and tissue paper colors that complement your decor.

SUPPLIES

Base:
White lampshade, 7" tall
Lamp base

Paper:
Bleeding tissue paper – Shades of blue and green
White card stock

Bead Tassel:
Bead mix – Blue and greens, 3mm to 6mm
Bugle beads, 1-1/4" long
Beading wire – two 20" pieces per tassel
Crimp beads

Tools & Other Supplies:
Decoupage medium, satin finish
Crimping tool

INSTRUCTIONS

Decorate the Shade:

1. Use the blue and green bleeding tissue paper to make color-transferred tissue. See the section on "Tissue Paper Collage" earlier in this book.

2. Cut rectangular pieces in a variety sizes (1" to 3" x 3/4") from the color-transferred tissue.

3. Using the photo as a guide, glue the tissue pieces to the lampshade using decoupage medium. (The placement is intentionally inexact for a whimsical mosaic effect.)

4. Cut narrow strips of tissue and glue them around the top and bottom edges of the lampshade, overlapping the pieces around the rims.

5. Cut smaller pieces as needed to fill in any empty spaces.

6. Coat the entire lampshade with decoupage medium. Let dry.

Make the Tassel:

1. Thread 7" of beads on both wire pieces. Thread one large bead over both ends of the wires, forming a loop.

2. Add 3-1/2" to 4" of beads to each of the four wires to form the ends of the tassel. At the end of each, place a crimp bead and crimp to secure. Trim off the excess wire. ❏

Joyful Memories
memory box

This box is decorated with a tissue paper collage and topped with an embellishment collage that uses scrapbooking elements. (These are easy to find.) If you like, you can substitute color-transferred tissue paper.

SUPPLIES

Base:

Papier mache box with lid,
  7-1/2" x 7-1/2" x 3"

Paper:

Tissue paper – Green, teal, blue

Embellishments:

Chipboard letters to spell JOY,
  2-1/2" to 3-1/2"

Clear and vellum sayings stickers

Rhinestone word sticker

Daisy stickers

1 yd. matching ribbon, 1/2" wide

Silver oval ribbon buckle

Tools & Other Supplies:

Acrylic paint – White

Decoupage medium, satin finish

Punches – Large starburst

Inkpad with silver ink

Rubber stamp – Swirl motif

Dimensional paint – Clear

Craft glue

Paint brush

Ruler

INSTRUCTIONS

Create the Collage:

1. Basecoat the box with white acrylic paint. Let dry.
2. Tear the tissue into strips, 1" to 3" wide.
3. Punch starburst shapes from tissue paper. TIP: To successfully punch the lightweight tissue, place three to four layers in the punch at one time.
4. Glue the strips to the box base and lid with decoupage medium, overlapping the pieces as you go and overlapping the edges of the box lid and base.
5. Glue the punched shapes randomly on the lid and sides of the box.
6. Coat the entire box – base and lid – with decoupage medium. Let dry.

Add the Embellishments:

1. Add the daisy stickers to the lid and sides.
2. Cover the chipboard letters with pieces of tissue paper, wrapping the tissue paper over the edges of the letters and securing on the backs. Let dry.
3. Stamp the letters, using the swirl stamp and silver ink.
4. Coat the letters with clear dimensional paint. Let dry.
5. Glue the letters on the top of the lid.
6. Add the saying stickers and rhinestone stickers.
7. Glue the ribbon and buckle around the sides of the lid. ❏

Beeswax Collage

This collage technique uses melted beeswax to adhere and protect the collage elements. It's perfect for beginners because it is easy to adjust and change the collage by re-heating the beeswax and moving the elements around. Beeswax is impervious to moisture and will not deteriorate. The finished collage is longlasting, has a beautiful amber luster, and smells faintly of honey. Since it takes about 1,000 flowers to make one drop of beeswax, a beeswax collage is a tribute to your talent and to the thousands of bees and flowers that produced the wax.

Pure beeswax may develop a white powdery surface (it's called "bloom") over time, especially if stored in a cool area. The bloom is your assurance of the purity of the wax. It can be removed by polishing the wax with a soft cloth or by heating it gently with a hair dryer.

Beeswax collages can be made on heavier-weight papers, canvas boards, or other rigid surfaces. You need about four ounces of beeswax for each square foot of collage. I like to use a smooth wooden board as a work surface.

The Beeswax Collage Technique

BASIC SUPPLIES

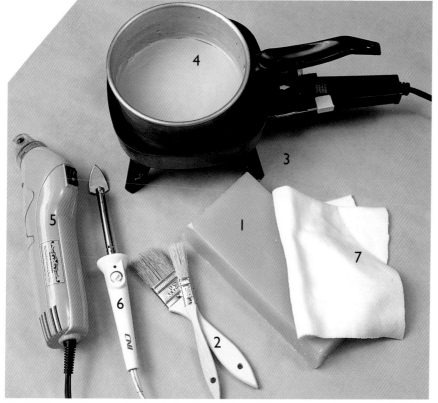

*1) 100% pure beeswax, 2) Bristle brushes, 1/2" and 1", 3) Electric frying pan, 4) Old pot **or** foil container, 5) Heat gun (the kind used for rubber stamp embossing), 6) Quilting iron, 7) Soft, lint-free polishing cloth*

INSTRUCTIONS

1. Place the beeswax in an old pot or a foil container.
2. Place the pot or container in the frying pan. Pour water around the container – it should be 1" deep. Add more water as needed as you are working. BE SAFE! Always use this double-boiler system when melting wax because wax is very flammable. **Never** leave the room while melting the wax or while the wax is over heat.
3. Place the base on a smooth wooden board. Brush the base with a layer of beeswax. Do not worry if it hardens. Do not be alarmed if the brushed wax has a creamy, opaque white color. As it hardens and cools, the wax turns a translucent amber color.
4. Place thin handmade paper, paper napkins, or tissue paper to create the background, brushing each piece to cover it with a layer of melted wax. The background paper(s) will become translucent, and you will be able to make some interesting effects with the layers. Keep adding paper pieces until the entire background and edges are covered. If, as you're working, you want to make a change in the placement of a paper piece or embellishment, simply heat the area with a heat gun, remove the paper,

and reposition it. Keep the heat gun at least 3" from the surface, and move it constantly – papers and embellishments can easily burn, scorch, or melt.
5. Continue creating your collage by adding additional papers and stickers to the base, coating each layer and element with wax.
6. Place embellishments such as dried flowers, leaves, or charms. Brush them with melted wax. Let cool and harden. TIP: Sometimes you need to let the collage cool up to an hour to view the final results.
7. When the collage is finished, smooth the wax and remove the brush strokes by heating the surface gently with the heat gun. Let cool and harden completely.
8. Polish the surface of the wax with a soft cloth. To clean up, simply let the brush and wax harden for your next beeswax collage project. The brush will soften when re-heated. ❑

Applying melted beeswax with a brush to a card.

Feathered Friends
cards

These beeswax collage cards use a friendly bird theme. The three examples show the variety of card colors, ribbons, charms, and cut motifs that can be used within one theme and with the same papers. Use the same technique with other theme ideas for a variety of unique cards to present to family and friends.

SUPPLIES

Base:

Blank cards, variety of natural hues, 4-1/4" x 5-1/2" (folded size)

Coordinating colors of card stock (for framing panels)

Heavy watercolor paper, cut into panels 4-1/2" x 5-1/2" (They will be trimmed after the collage is created to 3-1/2" x 4-3/4".)

Collage Papers:

Bird-theme tissue paper

Paper napkins with a bird theme

Decoupage paper with bird motifs (e.g., bird's nests or eggs)

Embellishments:

Feathers

Charms

Ribbon

Ribbon buckles

Tools & Other Supplies:

Basic supplies for beeswax collage (See the list at the beginning of this section.)

Scissors

Masking tape

Double-sided tape

INSTRUCTIONS

The instructions are for making one card, but you can make several at a time. For detailed instructions, see "The Beeswax Collage Technique."

1. Tape the watercolor paper panel to your work surface. (This helps to prevent the paper from warping while you work.)
2. Cut pieces of paper napkins and tissue paper. Cover the watercolor paper panel with a layer of beeswax. Apply the paper napkin piece. Layer with a piece of patterned tissue paper.
3. Cut bird-theme motifs from decoupage paper. Add the motifs.
4. Apply a feather, brushing the wax outward from the center so it keeps its shape.
5. Add the charm to the collage. Let cool and harden.
6. Trim the panel to 3-1/2" x 4-3/4", cutting off the masking tape.
7. Cut a framing panel 5" x 3-3/4" from a coordinating card stock. Use double-stick tape to adhere the beeswax collage panel to the card panel.
8. Wrap the ribbon and buckle around both panels and brush with wax to hold. Melt a little beeswax over the framing panel. (The paper will change color and darken where the wax is applied.)
9. Use double-sided tape to mount the collage to the front of the blank card.
10. Polish the card with soft cloth. ❑

"Sing and It Will Pass"
framed beeswax collage

A rustic frame and dried roses accent a beeswax collage created around the theme of a favorite saying. *"Canta che ti passa"* is Italian for "Sing and it will pass."

SUPPLIES

Base:

Canvas board, 11" x 14"

Natural wooden frame with 11" x 14" opening

Papers:

Tissue decoupage paper with flowers and script writing

Scrapbook paper with stone tiles

Scrapbook stickers of tiled letters

Scrapbook vintage letters

Saying stickers on clear backing

Pressed flowers *or* color photocopies of flowers (See "Making Your Own Flower Images for Collages.")

Postage stamp stickers with butterfly motifs

Skeleton leaves

Embellishments:

Silk roses

Label holder with computer-generated *or* lettered saying

Tools & Other Supplies:

Basic supplies for beeswax collage (See the list at the beginning of this section.)

Scissors

Small paper cups

Small nails

INSTRUCTIONS

1. Raise the canvas board 2" to 3" off your work surface with small paper cups.
2. Cover the canvas board with a layer of beeswax and apply the tissue decoupage paper. Take the paper over the edge and around to the back of the board, adhering with brushed beeswax.
3. Cut stone tiles cut from the scrapbook paper. Add the tile letter stickers to spell words on the tiles (e.g., "JOY," "BEAUTY")
4. Add saying stickers and postage stamp stickers.
5. Use vintage letter cutouts to spell out the main saying.
6. Accent with skeleton leaves and pressed flower images. Coat with a final layer of beeswax. Let cool and harden.
7. Polish with a soft cloth.
8. Insert the collage in the frame.
9. Accent the frame with dried or silk flowers (attach them with nails) and a label holder applied with beeswax. (The label holder frames the English translation of the saying.) ❏

Quilling

Quilling is the art of rolling or curling thin strips of paper into
different scrolled shapes and creating artistic designs with the various
shapes, which are then glued onto a base. Quilling is also known
as paper filigree or paper scroll work. Getting started in quilling
is easy and inexpensive. It requires few specialized tools, and
the techniques are suitable for any age group.

A quilled design can be simple, with a few coils, or a complex
masterpiece containing hundreds of individual coils and
scrolls. Quilled designs often include other paper techniques
such as fringing, crimping, and sculpted paper flowers,
which are nice additions to quilled arrangements.

Simple quilled cards can be made rather quickly, but many designs
take longer. More involved pieces can take hours of patient work
– an attraction of this paper craft. If you like to create unique,
carefully handmade cards and gifts, you will enjoy quilling.

Basic Supplies & Tools

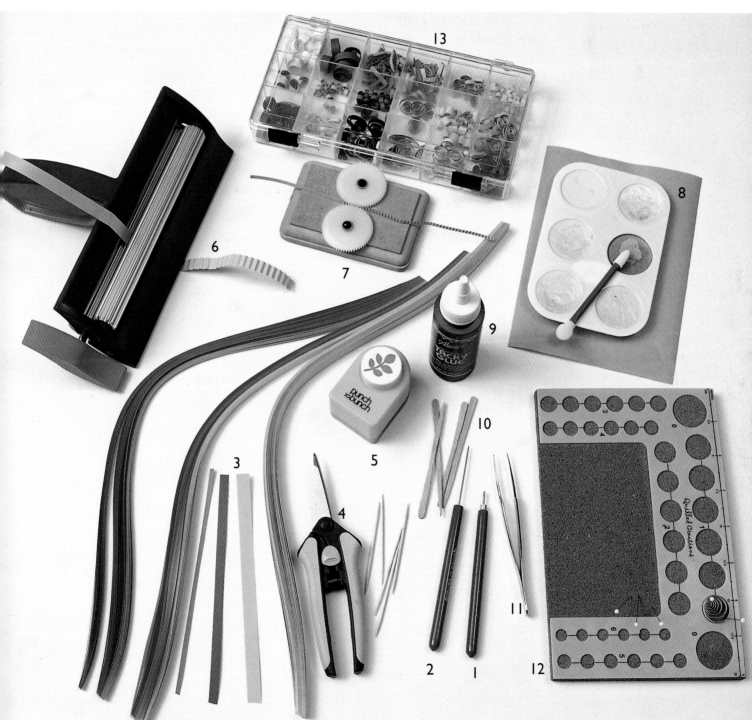

Pictured: 1) Quilling tool; 2) Needle tool; 3) Paper strips, 1/8", 1/4", 3/8"; 4) Scissors; 5) Punch; 6) Large paper crimper; 7) Paper crimper designed for quilling strips; 8) Watercolors; 9) White glue; 10) Toothpicks, flat and round; 11) Tweezers; 12) Quilling board with pins; 13) Storage container for quilled shapes

Basic Supplies & Tools

Pictured on page 63

QUILLING TOOL

A quilling tool has a metal shaft with a tiny slit in the middle that is mounted on a plastic or wooden handle. It makes it easy for beginners to roll the paper strips and create quilling shapes. Some tools have the manufacturer's name printed at the same place as the slit for easy location.

How to use a quilling tool:

1. Tear off a strip of quilling paper to the specified length. Slip the end of the paper into the slit and start rolling. TIP: It is easier to insert the paper if you hold it at a 45-degree angle to the tool.
2. Begin to roll the paper, using your fingers to maintain even tension and keep the strip even. You can roll the paper towards you or away from you; you will immediately discover which direction is natural for you.
3. When you reach the end of the paper strip, give the tool a one-quarter turn in the opposite direction to loosen it, and gently remove the coil. Simply let it expand to the size you want and glue the tail to secure.

NEEDLE TOOL

Many artists prefer a pointed end tool, like a paper piercer, for quilling paper. It is a little harder to master, but it makes a finer center hole in the shapes and tighter rolls. This needle tool is also used to make spirals. You can also use a round wooden toothpick instead of a needle tool to make coils.

How to use a needle tool:

1. Tear off a strip of quilling paper to the specified length. Slightly moisten one end of the strip and place the strip against your index finger. Place the pointed end of the tool on top of the end of the moistened strip. Place your thumb on top of the tool.
2. With the paper and tool now between your index finger and thumb, roll the paper around the tool, using your thumb. Keep the edges of the strip as even as possible as you roll the paper strip around the tool.

3. Remove the tool from the coil by simply pulling it out.

QUILLING PAPERS

Pre-cut paper strips 1/8" wide and 24" long are the most popular size for quilling. However, many other sizes are available. Look for 1/16", 3/8", 1/4", 1/2", 5/8", 3/4" and 1" widths. The 1/16" strips are used to make quilled designs in watches; the 3/8" strips are perfect for fringed flowers.

Quilling paper strips are readily available at crafts stores and come in a huge range of colors and types. They can be found in solid colored strips, graduated strips, center-graduated strips, two-toned strips, and metallic colored strips.

You can also make **your own specialized and custom strips**. You must be very accurate – the strip's width should be the same for the entire length. Use a paper trimmer and thin paper when cutting strips.

SCISSORS

Sharp, pointy scissors are what you need for trimming coils or for fringing. For easy and fast fringing, I especially like **spring-loaded ergonomic scissors**.

DECORATIVE PUNCHES

Leaf and branch motif punches can be used to quickly create foliage for quilled flower arrangements. Shape the leaves from the back on a **soft foam pad** with an **embossing tool** to create dimension before adding them to arrangements.

PAPER CRIMPER

A **paper crimper** adds another dimension to paper strips before quilling for a fanciful effect. You can use a crimper for both strips and paper panels. You can find small crimpers especially designed for quilling strips at crafts and stamping stores.

INTERFERENCE OR SHIMMERING IRIDESCENT WATERCOLORS

A light brushing of glistening paint adds a beautiful glimmer to quilled designs. Apply the paint over the shapes after gluing them to the base using very little moisture (too much could warp the paper shapes).

FRINGING MACHINE

A **fringing machine**, while expensive, cuts 3/8" paper strips into fringes evenly and quickly. If you are planning to make lots of fringed flower designs, this tool is recommended.

WHITE CRAFT GLUE

The best adhesive for quilling is **quick-drying white liquid glue** that dries clear. I like to pour the glue into a small disposable container and apply it with a toothpick. Stir the glue often or put a damp sponge over the top of the container to keep the glue from forming a film or drying out. (The sponge is also handy for keeping your fingers clean and free of glue.) TIP: Use a very small amount of glue when ending or joining your shaped coils – too much glue may show and spoil the look of your project.

WOODEN TOOTHPICKS

For applying glue, **flat toothpicks** work best. For rolling paper strips, use **round toothpicks**.

TWEEZERS

A good pair of **tweezers** is important for placing the paper coils. Use a sharp pointed set of tweezers for best results. Here's how: Hold the coil with tweezers, apply a small amount of glue to the bottom edges, and position.

You can also use tweezers when creating concentric coils to pull the centers of coils to the edge and for holding paper strips together tightly as the glue dries.

QUILLING BOARD

Although not essential, a **quilling board** is very handy for creating coils of the same size and for holding coils while the glue dries. Here's how: Place the rolled paper strip in the recessed hole of the board – the strip will release to the proper size. Use a pin to hold the loop to one side as you glue the end of the strip.

You could also use a **corkboard** to pin and hold the coils while they dry.

PINS

Use regular **straight pins** to hold your pieces together while the glue dries. They are also helpful for securing an arrangement when you want to set it aside to finish later.

BASES

Most quilled designs are arranged on paper cards, but you can also use surfaces such as **small canvas boards**, **wooden frames**, **journal covers**, or **paper tags** to showcase your work. Choose from the large selection of **embossed or window cards** with matching envelopes, or make your own card blanks.

I especially like **bubble cards** that come with a plastic dome to highlight the quilled design. The bubbles are available in different shapes, such a round, square, or rectangle.

WORK SPACE

A clean, well-lighted area is important when quilling. A **lamp** that mimics natural light is a good investment for this intricate work. Take frequent breaks and stretch your hands to avoid cramping.

STORING PAPER STRIPS & QUILLED SHAPES

Long, loose paper strips can quickly become damaged if they are not stored properly. I sort my strips by width and color and store them in their original plastic bag, held closed with a paper clamp. If you have space, hang up the bags for easy access.

I keep finished coils in segmented plastic containers sorted by size, type, and color. When I create coils and shapes for a project, I usually make a few extra of each one just in case. If I don't use them, these extra pieces are ready to use on other projects.

The Quilling Technique

1. **Prepare:** Choose your design, read the instructions carefully to make sure you have everything you need, and gather your supplies and tools.

2. **Tear:** Measure the paper strips with a ruler and tear the strips to the lengths specified in the project instructions. A torn edge can be glued better than a cut edge and will not create an obvious seam.

3. **Roll:** Start the first coil by threading the end of a paper strip through the slot in the metal tip of the quilling tool. (TIP: Hold the tool at an angle to the paper strip for easy threading.) Slide the tool to the very end of the strip and start to roll. Use your index and middle fingers to help guide the paper. Keep rolling until you reach the end of the strip. Move the tool a quarter twist back toward you. Gently wiggle the tool and pull it out of the coil.

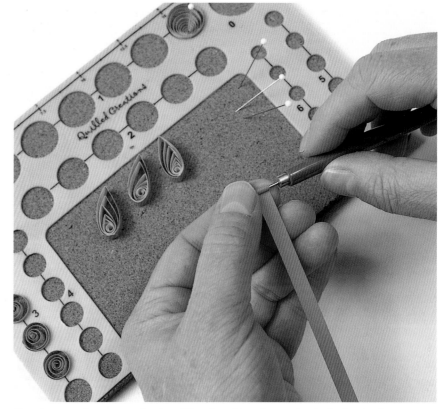

Starting to curl a paper strip. A quilling board can be seen in the background.

tips: QUILLING

• The tighter you roll the paper, the smaller the shape will be. • To make large shapes, glue two quilling strips together or attach two different colors.

• Be sure your coils are rolled evenly. I usually put my finger over the top as I roll to keep the edges even.

• Use very little glue – that's all you need to hold the pieces together.

• A needle tool creates a very fine hole in the center of tight coils; the slotted tool produces a tiny bent piece in the center. Always roll your quilling paper as close to the end as possible to minimize this crease.

To make a loose coil, set down the coil and release it. Pick up the coil, adjust the size, and put a tiny dot of glue inside the end. Press the end and hold for a few seconds to allow the glue to dry. *For tight coils,* leave the paper strip on the tool and glue the tail.

Create all your coils and shape them according to the instructions. As you go, pin the shapes to a quilling board to keep them organized *or* place a copy of the pattern on a corkboard, cover with a piece of wax paper, and pin the pieces in place.

4. **Arrange:** When you are happy with the arrangement, use very little glue to glue the coils together at the sides to create the designs.

5. **Attach:** To attach the quilled designs to the base, use a toothpick to apply a thin layer of glue to the bottom of the finished shape. ❑

Basic Quilled Shapes

With just a few shapes you can make a wide variety of quilled designs and cards. These are just a few of the many quilled shapes. Because the names of the shapes vary greatly within the quilling community, I have included alternative names in parentheses. These basic shapes are an excellent start for the beginner. With them, you will be able to create a wide variety of designs.

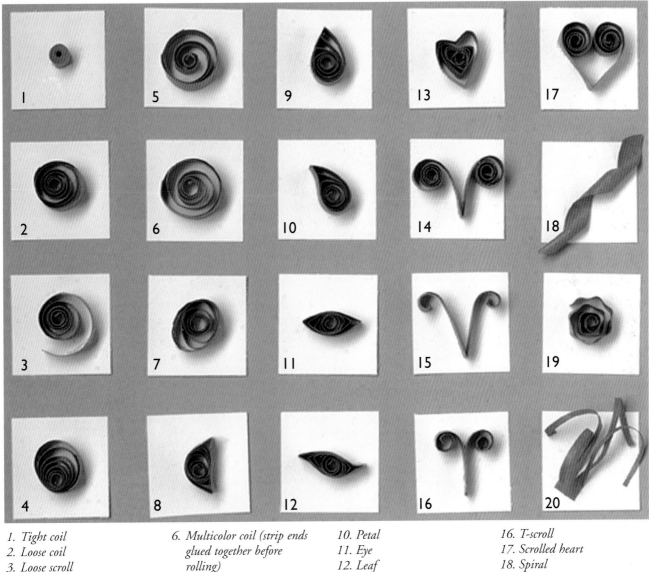

1. Tight coil
2. Loose coil
3. Loose scroll
4. Eccentric coil
5. Multicolor coil (strips rolled together)
6. Multicolor coil (strip ends glued together before rolling)
7. Oval
8. Half moon
9. Teardrop
10. Petal
11. Eye
12. Leaf
13. Heart
14. V-scroll
15. Feeler scroll
16. T-scroll
17. Scrolled heart
18. Spiral
19. Crimp
20. Scissors curl

Basic Quilled Shapes

Pictured on page 67

The circle is the shape that comes off the tool; it's the basic shape for all the others.

The size of the circle depends on the length of the paper and how tightly it is rolled.

1. Tight Coil (Peg) – Roll the strip. Glue closed while still on the quilling tool and the coil is tight. Remove carefully. Tight coils can be used as a design element or glued to the underside of another shape to raise it and create dimension.

2. Loose Coil – This is the most common, basic shape you make before pinching to create all the all other shapes. Roll the strip, remove it from quilling tool, and let it open. Place it in a circle template on a quilling board for a uniform size. Put a small amount of glue at the end to close.

3. Loose Scroll – Roll the strip, remove it from quilling tool, and let it open. (The tail is not glued.)

4. Eccentric Coil (Off-Center Coil) – Make a loose coil. Place it in a circle template on a quilling board and allow it to expand. Glue the end. Using a straight pin, pull the center of the coil off to the side and pin it to the board. Place a small amount of glue on top of the coiled edges to hold. Let dry, remove from board, and make the shape. Place the glue side down when arranging.

5. Multicolor Coil – Glue a strip of one color to the end of a strip of another color. Use as many colors as you want and roll as usual.

6. You can also make a multicolored coil by rolling two different strips at the same time. TIP: Offset the paper strips 1/4" at the beginning – two thicknesses of paper won't fit in the slot.

7. Oval – Make a loose coil. Squeeze gently into an oval shape without creasing the ends.

8. Half Moon – Make a loose coil. Pinch on two sides while placing your finger in the middle of one side – this will cause an indentation, creating the half moon shape.

9. Teardrop – Make a loose coil. Pinch one end of the circle to form the teardrop shape.

10. Petal – Make a loose coil, pinch one end of the circle to form as teardrop and as you pinch, twist slightly to make the curved petal.

11. Eye (Marquis Coil) – Make a loose coil. Pinch both ends of the circle.

12. Leaf – Make a loose coil. Pinch both ends of the circle, making an eye shape. As you pinch, twist the ends slightly to make the curved leaf shape.

13. Heart – Make a loose coil. Pinch one end as you do with the teardrop. Hold the pinched end in one hand while you push the other end towards the center to form the heart.

14. V-Scroll – Fold the strip in half. Roll the ends on the outside of the paper away from the inner crease.

15. Feeler Scroll – Roll a small part of the paper strip, leaving the rest of the strip straight. Feelers can be made with the strip folded in half (like this example) or with one coil from an unfolded strip.

16. T-scroll – Make a feeler scroll and glue the inside "legs" together.

17. Scrolled Heart (Open Heart) – Fold strip in half. Roll the ends toward the center of the crease to form the heart.

18. Spiral (Twist, Tendril) – Roll the paper strip in a spiral around the needle tool or toothpick.

19. Crimp (Waves) – For small waves, run the strip through a paper crimper. Roll the crimped strip into a loose coil. Shape the same as uncrimped strips.

20. Scissors Curl – Sometimes you want to put a slight curl in a paper strip. To do this, hold the scissors blade and paper strip flat against your thumb and gently pull the strip to curl. Repeat for more curl. TIP: Hold the blade gently to avoid ripping the paper.

Fringed Flowers

Supplies for Making Fringed Flowers

- Quilling strips, 3/8" wide x 6" long paper strip per flower, or fringed strips (cut the strip length shorter or longer to vary the flower size, or wider 1/4" and 3/4" paper strips to make the flowers bigger) Shaded quilling papers are especially nice. A nice variation is to trim the paper strip before fringing with decorative scissors.
- Sharp scissors with short blades
- Fringing tool
- Quilling tool
- Decorative edge scissors (optional)

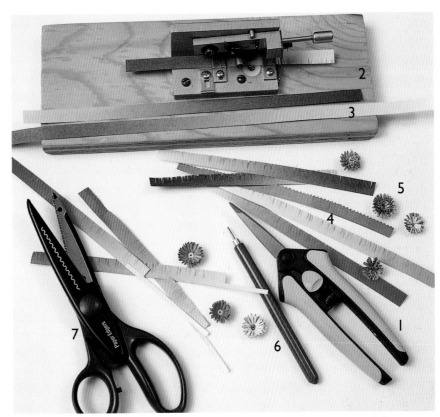

1) Scissors; 2) Fringing tool; 3) Quilling strips; 4) Fringed strips; 5) Fringed flowers; 6) Quilling tool; 7) Decorative edge scissors

Making a different-colored center for a fringed flower.

Making Fringed Flowers

Here's how to make a fringed flower without a fringing tool:

1. For easier fringing, draw a light pencil line along the long edge of a 3/8" paper strip, 1/8" from the edge. Use this line as a cutting guide.
2. Make small cuts very close together, evenly spaced, up to the cutting guideline. (This is fringing.)
3. After the strip is fringed, roll it up into a tight coil and glue the end.
4. Holding the flower between both thumbs and index fingers, peel the fringed petals outward with your thumbs. Voila! A fringed flower!
5. To create a center for the fringed flower, leave 1" to 2" unfringed at the beginning of the strip. Trim the unfringed part of the strip to 1/8" wide, and start rolling from this end. This will form a tight center in the flower.
6. To make a flower with a different-colored center. Cut a 1" paper strip 1/8" wide of the color you want the center to be. Glue to the fringed strip as shown in the photo.

SUPPLIES FOR MAKING SWIRL FLOWERS

Pictured: 1) Swirl stamps (available in five sizes for flowers 1/2" to 1"
in diameter); 2) Card weight paper with stamped images
(Choose paper in flower colors.); 3) Inkpads;
4) Scissors; 5) Decorative edge scissors;
6) Hemostat (metal clamp);
7) Glue gun with clear glue sticks

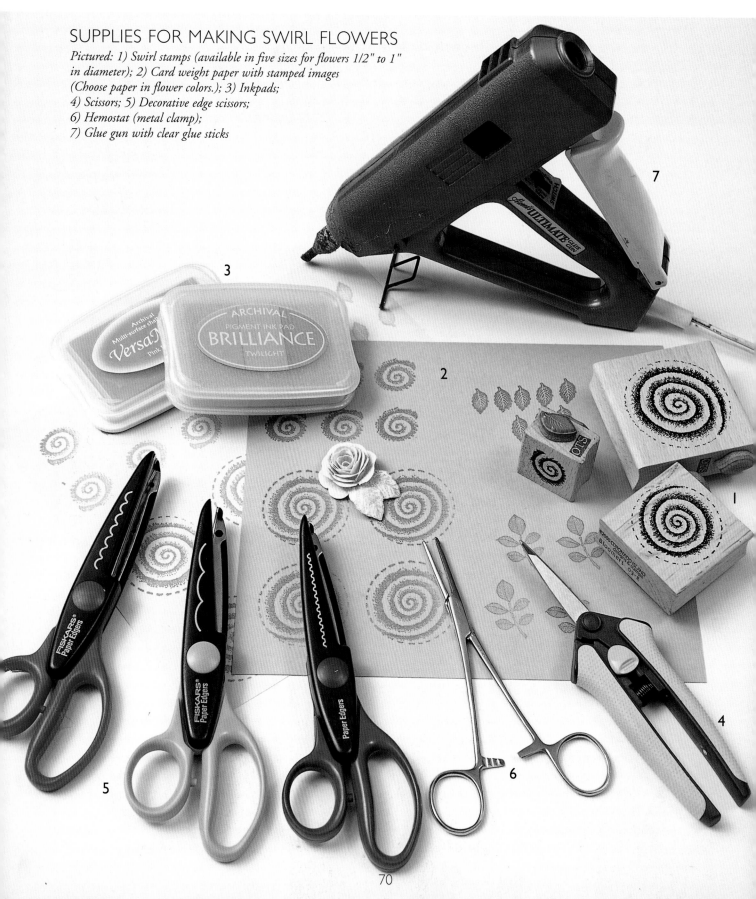

Swirl Flowers

These sculpted paper flowers are a wonderful addition to quilled arrangements, and using the specially designed rubber stamps makes it easy to create these miniature paper beauties. The same company that designed the stamps also makes a variety of vase and branch stamps. For an endless variety of blooms, try changing the paper, ink colors, decorative scissors, and swirl size.

Making Swirl Flowers

1. Using the stamp and inkpad, stamp a sheet of swirls.

2. With decorative scissors, start cutting the swirl from the outside to the center, following the swirl design. (Photo 1) Keep the scissors in one place and move the paper, feeding it into the blades. As you cut, line up the cut motifs with the blades so they fit like puzzle pieces.

3. Clamp the hemostat (metal clamp) on the outside tip of the swirl. Remove your fingers from the clamp handles and, holding the stem (Photo 2), roll the paper towards the center of the swirl, keeping the edges even.

4. Open the jaws of the metal clamp and gently remove it. Let the rolled paper strip open into a flower shape.

Photo 1 – Cutting out the swirl with decorative scissors.

Photo 2 – Twirling the cut swirl around a hemostat (metal clamp).

Continued on the next page

Making Swirl Flowers, continued.

5. Adjust the bloom as desired (Photo 3).

6. Turn it over. Hold the flower so you can see the hole in the middle. Apply a generous drop of hot glue and press the base at the center to cover the hole. Before the glue completely sets, use the metal clamp to arrange the blossom, rolling and repositioning the center.

Photo 3 – A finished, formed rose before gluing.

Making Swirl Roses: Use plain scallop, large scallop, or pinked scalloped decorative edge scissors to trim the edge of paper. Use the metal clamp to further shape the individual petals by grasping and rolling them slightly. See examples in the photo of the finished roses.

Making Swirl Zinnias: Cutting the swirl with tiny motif decorative scissors (e.g., tiny scallop, tiny pinking) creates zinnia-type blossoms. After you cut out the swirl, cut a fringe along the edge with straight scissors, using the scissors motifs as guides. Then roll and form the blossom.

Example A – Zinnia-type blossoms cut with tiny scallop, tiny pinking, and stamp edge decorative scissors, using a variety of paper and inkpad colors.

Example B – A variety of roses cut with different decorative scissors using a variety of paper and inkpad colors.

Example C – Two roses showing the variation achieved with one pair of decorative scissors. I used the same large scalloped-edge scissors for both roses – one was cut with the rounded scallop up; the other has the pointed edge of the scallop up.

Shaped Foliage

Supplies for Foliage

Card stock

Leaf stamp for foliage

Inkpad

Embossing mat (A thin foam pad or mouse pad will work.)

Scissors

Embosser (This is a nylon shaping tool; a spoon-shaped or large ball metal embosser could be used.)

Adhesive (this can be a glue gun with clear glue sticks, silicone glue, or glue dots. I prefer to use a generous drop of hot glue – it preserves the shape of the paper piece and gives it a raised appearance. Be careful not to use so much glue that it shows on the finished design.

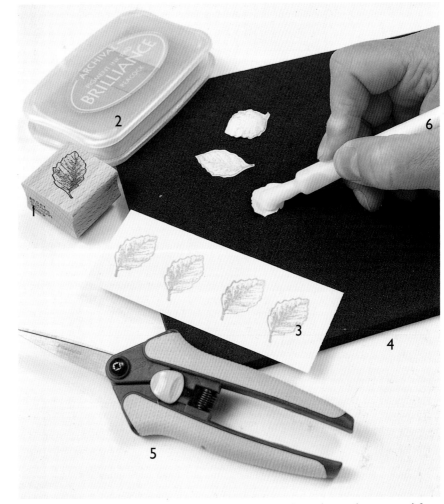

Using an embosser to shape paper pieces. The photo also shows the supplies you need for shaping paper pieces:
1) Leaf stamp; 2) Inkpad; 3) Stamped images; 4) Embossing mat (A thin foam pad or mouse pad will work.); 5) Scissors; 6) Embosser (This is a nylon shaping tool; a spoon-shaped or large ball metal embosser could be used.)

Making Shaped Foliage

1. Using a leaf stamp and green ink, stamp leaf images on cardstock weight paper.
2. Cut out the stamped image with scissors.
3. Place the paper cutout, stamped side down, on the embossing pad. Press the paper embosser into the cutout and shape the paper by pressing in a circular motion. (The cutout will become a curved, raised shape.)
4. Attach the shape to your surface with your chosen adhesive.

Olives, Suds & Bubbles
party cards

These bold designs use only a few quills to accent the design. They are
an introduction to quilling for a beginner. The placement of the
paper elements is loose for a whimsical touch.

SUPPLIES

Base: Black card, 8" x 5"

Papers:
Black panel, 3" x 3-3/4"
Metallic red, 3-1/2" x 4-1/2"
Plain vellum
Silver metallic
Red
Green

Tools & Other Supplies:
Basic tools and supplies for quilling
(See the beginning of this section.)
Double-sided tape
White craft glue
Bone folder
Paper trimmer

SUPPLIES

Base: Black card, 8" x 5"

Papers:
Black panel, 3" x 3-3/4"
Metallic gold patterned panel,
3-1/2" x 4-1/2"
Copper metallic paper
Plain vellum • White

Tools & Other Supplies:
Basic tools and supplies for quilling
(See the beginning of this section.)
Double-sided tape • White craft glue
Bone folder • Paper trimmer

SUPPLIES

Base:
Black card, 6" x 6-3/4"

Papers:
Black panel, 2" x 5-1/2"
Metallic gold patterned panel,
2-1/2" x 6"
Gold metallic
Plain vellum

Tools & Other Supplies:
Basic tools and supplies for quilling
(See the beginning of this section.)
Double-sided tape • White craft glue
Bone folder • Paper trimmer

The Martini Card

INSTRUCTIONS

Make the Background:
1. Fold and crease the black card with a bone folder to 4" x 5".
2. Trim the edges of the black and metallic red paper panels at random angles to form the irregular rectangle shapes.
3. Cut a martini glass from plain vellum. Cut a triangle for the martini from silver metallic paper.
4. Arrange and attach the panels and cut pieces to the card front using double-sided tape. TIP: Place the tape on the vellum where the paper pieces on top will prevent the tape from showing.

Add the Quilled Olives:
Make four. See the beginning of this section for detailed instructions.
1. Cut the red and green paper into 1/4" wide strips. Cut the red strip into 4" lengths. Cut the green strips into 6" lengths. Glue the ends of one red strip to one green strip.
2. Start rolling a tight coil at the red end and glue to hold. Continue, rolling the green strip into a loose coil. Form into an eccentric coil and shape into an oval. Glue to the card with white craft glue. Let dry. ❑

The Beer Card

INSTRUCTIONS

Make the Background:
1. Fold and crease the black card with a bone folder to 4" x 5".
2. Trim the edges of the black and metallic gold paper panels at random angles to form the irregular rectangle shapes.
3. Cut a beer glass cut from plain vellum. Cut the beer from copper metallic paper.
4. Arrange and attach the panels and cut pieces to the card front using double-sided tape. TIP: Place the tape on the vellum where the paper pieces on top will prevent the tape from showing.

Add the Quilled Beer Suds:
Make 10 to 11. See the beginning of this section for detailed instructions.
1. Cut the white paper into strips 1/4" wide. Cut the strips into 3" and 4" lengths.
2. Shape into loose scrolls. Glue to the card with white craft glue. Let dry. *Variation:* Stack more suds on top for a frothier, three-dimensional effect. ❑

The Champagne Card

INSTRUCTIONS

Make the Background:
1. Fold and crease the black card with a bone folder to 3" x 6-3/4".
2. Trim the edges of the black and metallic gold paper panels at random angles to form the irregular rectangle shapes.
3. Cut two champagne glasses from plain vellum. Cut the champagne from gold metallic paper.
4. Arrange and attach the panels and cut pieces to the card front using double-sided tape. TIP: Place the tape on the vellum where the paper pieces on top will prevent the tape from showing.

Add the Quilled Champagne Bubbles:
Make 3 to 4 loose coils and 1 to 2 tight coils per glass. See the beginning of this section for detailed instructions.
1. Cut 1/4" wide strips from plain vellum. Cut into 2" to 3" lengths.
2. Quill into loose coils and tight coils. Use white glue to attach the quilled shapes to the card. Let dry. ❑

SUPPLIES

Base:

Pink embossed card blank, 4" x 6" (folded size)

Papers:

Pink origami panel, 5-3/4" x 3-3/4"

Light beige panel, 5-1/2" x 3-1/2"

Quilling strips, 1/8" – Pinks, greens, pale yellow

Quilling strips, 3/8" – Pale yellow

Tools & Other Supplies:

Basic tools and supplies for quilling and shaping (See the beginning of this section.)

Rubber stamp – Branch motif, Asian characters, Asian seal

Inkpads – Light brown, black

Double-sided tape

White craft glue

Mini punch – Flower

3 bamboo clips

Cherry Blossoms
card

This quilled design uses stamped branches as guides for arranging the quilled leaves and blossoms. Different shades of quilling strips are used to make the cherry blossoms for variety. You can make a Dogwood Blossom Card by using cream paper for the blossoms.

INSTRUCTIONS

Decorate the Card Base:

1. Stamp the branch, characters, and seal on the light beige panel.
2. Using double-sided tape, mount the stamped panel and origami panel to the card front.

Make the Quilled Shapes:

See the beginning of this section for detailed instructions.

1. Blossoms (5 petals per flower, 3 flowers per card) – Cut 4" lengths of different shades of pink paper strips. Shape into fat teardrops.
2. Blossom Centers (1 per flower) – Cut 3" lengths of pale yellow paper strips. Shaped into tight coils. Punch small flowers from 3/8" a pale yellow paper strip. Emboss to shape.

3. Flower Buds (4 buds per card) – Cut 4" lengths of different shades of pink paper strips. Shape into fat teardrops.
4. Calyxes (1 per bud) – Cut 3" lengths of different shades of green paper strips. Shape into hearts.
5. Leaves (20 to 22 per card) – Cut 4" lengths of light and medium green paper strips. Shape into leaves.

Assemble:

1. Glue the blossoms and blossom centers together.
2. Using the stamped branches as guides, glue the blossoms, buds, and leaves in place with white glue. Let dry.
3. Cut tiny slits in the top fold and insert the bamboo clips. ❑

Bamboo Garden
card

Quilling paper strips are used for the stalks and act as guides for arranging the quilled leaves. Different shades of quilling strips are used for the bamboo leaves for variety.

SUPPLIES

Base:
Olive green linen card blank,
  6-3/4" x 4-1/2" (folded size)

Papers:
Bamboo vellum panel, 4" x 6-1/2"
Light green embossed panel,
  6" x 3-1/2"
Shaded green quilling strips, 1/4"
  and 1/8"
Light and medium green quilling
  strips, 1/8"

Tools & Other Supplies:
Glue stick
Double-sided tape
White craft glue
Three bamboo clips

INSTRUCTIONS

Decorate the Card Base:
1. Cut 1" to 1-3/4" pieces of 1/4" and 1/8" shaded green quilling strips for the stalk sections.
2. Using the glue stick, glue the pieces of shaded quilling paper on the light green embossed panel to form the bamboo stalks.
3. Using double-sided tape, mount the stalk panel and vellum panel on the card front.

Make the Quilled Elements:
See the beginning of this section for detailed instructions.
Bamboo leaves (30 to 32 per card) – Cut the 1/8" wide light and medium green strips into 2" to 6" lengths. Shape into eyes with no curled tips. Pinch firmly so they are long and pointed.

Finish:
1. Using the photo as a guide, glue the leaves.
2. Cut tiny slits in the side fold and insert the bamboo clips. ❏

Garden Sampler
framed wall piece

This delightful sampler uses simple quilled shapes to create a variety of elements. You can use these quilled designs individually or in groups to make cards and tags.

SUPPLIES

Base:
Wooden frame with 5 windows, 8-1/2" x 9-1/4"
Piece of foam core board to fit frame, 7-1/2" x 8-1/4"

Papers:
Muted green decorative papers in different patterns
Green
Quilling strips, 1/8" wide – Black, yellow, cream, orange, red, purple, bright green, dark green,
Quilling strips, 3/8" wide – Light green, medium green

Embellishments:
Garden theme rub-on
Jute string
Charms – Mini watering can, shovel

Tools & Other Supplies:
Basic tools and supplies for quilling and shaping (See the beginning of this section.)
Paper trimmer
Glue stick
White craft glue
Acrylic paint – Antique white
Sandpaper, 100 grit
Acrylic varnish, matte finish
Pencil
Small nails
Paper punch – Fern, leaf
Stamps – Leaf, swirl
Inkpad – Green

INSTRUCTIONS

Prepare:
1. Basecoat the frame with antique white paint. Let dry.
2. Sand to distress. Wipe away dust.
3. Apply a coat of matte varnish. Let dry.
4. Accent the frame with the garden rub-on.
5. Place the foam core piece in the frame. With a pencil, lightly mark the window openings.
6. Using the pencil marks, measure and cut the pieces of decorative paper 1/4" larger than the openings.
7. Remove the foam core. Glue the paper pieces to the foam core with a glue stick. Replace the foam core in the frame.
8. Using small nails and white glue, attach the jute string to the frame to make a hanger.
9. Glue the watering can in place. Tie on the shovel with a piece of jute.

Make the Bumblebees:
Bumblebee Head (1 per bee) – Cut a 4" black paper strip. Shape into a half moon.
Bumblebee Body (1 per bee) – Cut 6" each black and yellow paper strips. Roll at the same time to shape a multicolored eccentric coil. Form into a slight oval.
Bumblebee Wings (2 per bee) – Cut 6" cream paper strip. Shape into a teardrop.
Bumblebee Feelers (1 per bee) – Cut a 2" black paper strip. Shape into feelers.

Make the Carrots:
Carrot – Cut an 8" orange paper strip. Shape into an eccentric coil. Form into a long teardrop.
Carrot Greenery (1 pair per carrot) – Punch the fern shape from light and medium green 3/8" strips.

Make the Radishes:
Radish – Cut a 6" red paper strip. Shape into a teardrop.
Radish Greenery – (1 of each per radish) Punch leaf and fern shapes from light and medium green 3/8" strips.

Make the Eggplant:
Eggplant – Cut a 12" purple paper strip. Shape into an eccentric coil. Form into a lopsided oval.

Eggplant Greenery – Cut 1" and 1-1/2" lengths of green strips. Fold in half. Curl with scissors.

Eggplant Leaf – Stamp leaf on green paper with green ink. Cut out. Shape with an embossing tool.

Make the Peas:

Peas – Cut 5", 6", and 7" lengths of bright green paper strips. Form into tight coils for a variety of pea sizes.

Peapod – Cut 2" and 2-1/2" pieces of dark green strips. Wrap around peas to form pod. Make curls at top.

Make the Onions:

Green Onion Bulb – Cut a 6" length of gray paper strip. Shape into an eye. Cut two 1-1/4" lengths of gray paper strips. Fringe with 1/4" cuts at one end. Curl the other end with scissors.

Onion Greenery – Cut two 4" lengths of green strips. Fold in half and curl slightly with scissors.

To assemble the green onion: Glue the fringed gray pieces on either side of the eye shape with the fringe (the root) at the bottom. Glue the green pieces in the center to form the top. Trim the greenery at different lengths to finish.

Make the Cabbage:

Cabbage – Stamp a swirl on green paper with green ink. Cut out. Assemble as you would a rose to a 1" diameter.

Finish:

1. Glue the quilled pieces together to form the individual motifs.

2. Glue in place in the frame with white glue. Refer to the project photo for placement ideas. ❑

Quilled Dragonflies
pins

Coating quilled shapes with a polymer coating makes them strong and waterproof – perfect for wearable art! Each pin measures 2-1/2" x 2". These instructions are for the dragonfly with light green and light blue wings (the upper one in the photo). You can vary the look by changing the colors of the papers used for the wings.

SUPPLIES

Paper:

Quilling paper strips, 1/8" wide – Purple, dark green, light blue, light green

Tools & Other Supplies:

Polymer coating supplies (See the beginning of the Collage section for a list.)

Basic tools and supplies for quilling and shaping (See the beginning of this section.)

Pin back

Interference watercolors

Rhinestones – one 6mm, five 4mm, two 3mm

Jewelry glue

INSTRUCTIONS

Make the Pieces:

1. Eyes (2 per dragonfly) – Cut 4" lengths of purple paper strips. Shape into tight coils.
2. Body (1 per dragonfly) – Cut one 2" length, two 4" lengths, two 6" lengths, and one 12" length of dark green paper strips. Shape into tight coils. Glue coils together from large to small in a slightly curved line.
3. Tail (1 per dragonfly) – Cut one 2-1/2" length of dark green paper strip. Fold in half. Shaped into a "feeler."
4. Wings (2 of each color per dragonfly) – Cut two 10" lengths of light blue and two 12" lengths of light green paper strips. Roll into eccentric coils. Shape into long teardrops.

Assemble:

1. Glue the eyes to the top of the body shape. Glue the tail to the end of the body. Slightly curve the tail to follow the curve of the body.
2. Glue the wings to the body at the top of the body just under the eyes.
3. Brush watercolors on the wings. Let dry.
4. Brush all the paper pieces with two coats of thin white glue to seal them. Let dry completely.
5. Coat the dragonfly with polymer coating. See "Basic Steps for Applying a Polymer Coating" for instructions. When the polymer coating has cured for a few hours and is still tacky, place the rhinestones on the body and eyes. Let cure completely.
6. Glue the pin back in place with jewelry glue. ❏

Bouquets of Greetings
floral cards

These four floral card designs show a variety of possibilities for using quilling, fringed flowers, swirl flowers, and crimped flowers.

Pictured clockwise from top left: Crimped Flowers Card, Bubble Window Card, Rose Topiary Card, Zinnia Vase Card.

Instructions begin on page 82.

Zinnia Vase

Pictured on page 81

The rubber stamp company that designed the swirl flower stamps also has leaf designs that correspond with punches. You simply stamp the leaf motifs and punch out the shapes. If you do not have the punch, you can hand cut the individual leaves.

SUPPLIES

Base:
Lavender card, 4-1/2" x 6" (folded size)

Papers:
Beige card panel, 4" x 5-1/2"
Green metallic panel, 4-1/4" x 5-3/4"
White card stock
Lavender (for swirl flowers)
Purple (for swirl flowers)
Quilling strips, 3/8" wide – Shaded blue, shaded purple, purple

Tools & Other Supplies:
Basic tools and supplies for quilling and shaping (See the beginning of this section.)

Decorative edge scissors – Mini pinking, stamp
Iris crystal seed beads
Dimensional paint – Clear
Inkpads – Dark green, light green metallic, light lilac, black
Decorative punches – Small leaf, small branch
Rubber Stamps – Small swirl flower, medium swirl flower, large swirl flower, flowers and vase, crackle texture
Double-sided tape
White craft glue
Glue gun and clear glue sticks

INSTRUCTIONS

Make the Base:
1. Stamp the flowers and vase motif on the beige panel.
2. Mount the beige panel on the metallic green panel. Trim with mini pinking decorative scissors.
3. Mount those panels on the front of the lavender card blank.

Make the Flowers:
1. Blue Fringe Flowers – Cut 6" lengths of shaded blue 3/8" quilling paper. Make two blue fringed flowers.
2. Purple Fringe Flowers – Cut 6" lengths of shaded and solid purple hued 3/8" quilling paper. Make three fringed flowers.
3. Swirl Flowers – Make a variety of zinnias, using the small, medium, and large swirl stamps with lavender and purple paper. Cut out the swirls with stamp edge decorative scissors.

Stamp & Punch:
1. Cut the vase motif from white card stock. Stamp with the crackle design.
2. Shade the edges of the vase with the light lilac inkpad. Shape the vase on an embossing pad.
3. Color white card paper with light green metallic ink. Stamp the leaves using dark green ink. Punch or cut out.
4. Use light green metallic ink to color white paper. Punch out small branches.

Assemble:
1. Glue the flowers, leaves, shaped vase, and punched branches with hot glue.
2. Glue seed beads on the ends of the branches and in flower centers with white craft glue
3. Coat the vase with clear dimensional paint. ❏

Bubble Window Card

Pictured on page 81

SUPPLIES

Base:
Cream card, 4" x 6" (folded size), with round window and plastic bubble

Papers:
Lime green paper panel, 3-1/2" x 5-1/2"
Quilling paper strips, 3/8" wide – Shaded pink
Quilling paper strips, 1/8" wide – Green

Tools & Other Supplies:
Basic tools and supplies for quilling and shaping (See the beginning of this section.)
Rhinestone stickers
Peel off stickers – Silver swirls, leaves, "thank you"
Double-sided tape
Glue gun and glue sticks

INSTRUCTIONS

Make the Quilled Elements:
1. Fringe Flowers – Cut 6" lengths of shaded pink 3/8" paper strips. Make three flowers. Roll from both the dark and light ends for variety. Add rhinestones in the centers of two flowers.
2. Tendrils – Crimp the green paper strips. Cut 2" lengths and make three "feelers."

Assemble:
1. Place sliver sticker swirls and leaves at the center of the green panel.
2. Using hot glue, attach the fringed flowers and green "feelers."
3. Place the plastic bubble in the window. Adhere the green panel inside of card with tape, centering the design in the window.
4. Add additional silver swirls and the "thank you" sticker to the front of the card. ❏

Crimped Flowers Card

Crimping the quilling strips before forming the shapes is a fun variation. Try crimping the paper on other quilled designs for a different, quirky look.

SUPPLIES

Base:

Bright blue card, 3-1/2" x 5-3/4" (folded size)

Papers:

Lime green card stock

Turquoise card panel, 3" x 5"

Purple card panel, 3-1/4" x 5-1/2"

Quilling strips, 1/8" wide – Light green, medium green, blue, purple

Green metallic paper cord

Tools & Other Supplies:

Basic tools and supplies for quilling and shaping (See the beginning of this section.)

Dimensional paints – Purple, blue, clear

Paper crimper

Double-sided tape

White craft glue

Glue gun and glue sticks

Rubber stamp – Flowers and vase

Inkpad – Black

INSTRUCTIONS

Make the Base:

1. Stamp the flowers and vase motif on the turquoise panel and stamp the vase on lime green card paper with black ink.
2. Use the paper crimper to crimp the purple card panel. Mount the turquoise panel on the purple panel.
3. Mount the panels on the front of the card.
4. Cut out the stamped vase on the lime green card stock. Shape on an embossing mat. Glue in place with hot glue.

Make the Quilled Elements:

Crimp all the paper strips before rolling into the shapes.

1. Leaves – Cut 6" lengths of light and medium green paper strips. Make five leaves.
2. Buds – Cut 6" lengths of blue and purple paper strips. Make seven buds.
3. Flowers – Cut 7" lengths of blue and purple paper strips. Make two scrolled hearts.
4. Calyxes – Cut 3" lengths of green paper strips. Fold in half. Make two "feelers."

Assemble:

1. Cut small pieces of metallic paper cord for the stems and stamen.
2. Glue the paper cord, flowers, buds, calyxes, and leaves with white glue.
3. With the colored dimensional paints, add details to the vase and accents to the flower arrangement. Let dry completely.
4. Paint the vase with clear dimensional paint. Let dry. ❏

Rose Topiary Card

Pictured on page 81

SUPPLIES

Base:

Light rose card, 3-1/2" x 6-3/4" (folded size)

Papers:

Dark green card panel, 3-1/4" x 6-1/4"

Rose metallic paper panel, 3-1/2" x 6-1/2"

Black card paper

Pink

Lavender

White

Tools & Other Supplies:

Basic tools and supplies for quilling and shaping (See the beginning of this section.)

Rubber stamps – Rose topiary, leaf, small swirl, medium swirl, pink, lavender

Inkpads – Metallic light green, metallic gold

Interference watercolors

Decorative edge scissors – Deckle

Double-sided tape

Glue gun

Paint brush

INSTRUCTIONS

Prepare the Card:

1. Stamp the rose topiary on the dark green panel with metallic green ink and on the black card paper with gold ink.
2. Mount the dark green panel on the rose metallic panel. Trim with deckle edge scissors.
3. Mount the panels on the front of the card.

Continued on next page

Rose Topiary Card, continued

4. Cut out the stamped pot and shape on an embossing mat.

Make the Topiary Elements:
1. Leaves – Stamp the motifs on white paper with light green metallic ink. Cut out and shape.
2. Swirl roses – Make a variety of small and medium roses using the swirl stamps on pink and lavender paper. Cut out with large and medium scallop scissors.

Assemble:
1. Glue the shaped vase in place with a glue gun.
2. Glue the shaped leaves, then the roses with hot glue.
3. Brush the watercolors on the tips of the roses to tint the petals. ❏

Olives & Cranberries
wall panels

SUPPLIES

Bases:
2 stretched canvases, 4" x 6" x 3/4"

Papers:
Card stock – Dark green, olive green

2 decorative paper panels, 5-3/4" x 3-3/4"

Quilling paper strips, 1/8" wide – Olive green, tan (for the Cranberry Panel), dark green, brown (for the Olive Panel)

Tools & Other Supplies:
Basic tools and supplies for quilling and shaping (See the beginning of this section.)

Acrylic paint – Dark plum

Brush

Inkpad – Brown

Copper wire, 22 gauge

Oval beads – 5 black (for the Olive Panel), 4 wine-colored (for the Cranberry Panel)

Double-sided tape

White glue

Needlenose pliers

INSTRUCTIONS

Make the Quilled Shapes:
See the beginning of this section for detailed instructions. Using different lengths creates a variety of leaf sizes.
1. Cut 3" to 5" lengths of green paper strips. Shape into leaves.
2. Glue a 3" length of brown or tan paper strip to each leaf for a stem.
3. Construct the branches, starting at the top and gluing the stem pieces together. Layer a few leaves without stems on top of the branches for a three-dimensional effect.

Prepare the Panels:
1. Basecoat the canvas with dark plum acrylic paint. Let dry.
2. Tape the decorative paper panel on the canvas.
3. Cut 2" x 3" diamond shapes from the card stock (olive green for the Olive Panel, dark green for the Cranberry Panel). Shade the edges with brown ink.
4. Tape the diamond shapes to the decorative paper, using the photo as a guide for placement.

Assemble:
1. With white glue, mount the branches on the canvas.
2. Cut a 2" to 3" length of copper wire for each bead. Form a tiny loop on one end of each piece of wire.
3. Thread a bead on each wire stem and gently curve the wire. Dip the wire end in glue and place on the branch. Let dry. Repeat until all the beads are attached.
4. Adjust the beads and glue to hold in place. ❏

By changing the leaf and bead colors, you can make an olive branch or a cranberry branch.
The Cranberry Panel has olive green leaves with tan branches and wine beads;
the Olive Panel has dark green leaves with brown branches and black beads.
A mistletoe panel is another variation: Use pale green leaves, green stems, and white beads
for a holiday panel. These quilled designs could also adorn cards or book covers
or be used as a design element on a scrapbook page.

Flowers in a Dome
quilled journal cover

Here, a plastic bubble highlights and protects the quilled design. Using a bubble is a good idea for the front of a journal that will get lots of use as a guest book or memory album.

SUPPLIES

Base:
Blue embossed coil-bound journal, 7" x 7-1/2" with a 2-1/2" square window in the front cover
Round plastic bubble, 3"

Paper:
Card stock – Light blue, pink, dusty purple, dusty pink embossed
Quilling paper strips, 1/8" wide – Purple, olive green
Quilling paper strips, 3/8" wide – Shaded purple
Quilling paper strips, 1/4" wide – Shaded purple

Tools & Other Supplies:
Basic tools and supplies for quilling and shaping (See the beginning of this section.)
Interference watercolors
Decorative edge scissors – Deckle
Rhinestones, 4mm – Pink, blue, green
6 clear rhinestones, 3mm
1/2 yd. pink wire-edge ribbon, 3/8" wide
Shape cutter
Circle nesting template
Cutting mat
Paper trimmer
Decorative corner punch
Double-sided tape
White craft glue
Paint brush

INSTRUCTIONS

Cut the Papers:
Using the paper trimmer, shape cutter, and circle template, cut these pieces:
• A 3-1/2" square light blue card stock panel with a 2-1/2" round window
• A 4-1/4" square pink card stock panel with a 3-1/2" round window and decoratively punched corners
• A 4" square dusty purple card stock panel with a 3" round window and decoratively punched corners
• A 6-1/2" square dusty pink floral embossed card panel

Make the Quilled Elements:
1. Daisy Flowers (make 2) – Cut 6" long strips from 1/8" wide purple paper. For each flower, make 5 quilled teardrops and a tight coil center.
2. Fringe Flowers (make 3) – Cut 6" strips. Use shaded purple 3/8" and 1/4" paper strips. Trim the light purple strips with deckle edge scissors before fringing.
3. Leaves (make 10) – Make leaf shapes from 1/8" wide x 3"-5" long olive green paper strips. Vary the lengths of the strips for various size leaves.
4. Curled branches with buds – Make "feelers" from 1/8" wide x 2" long olive green paper strips. Add 1/8" wide x 1" long purple paper strips rolled into tight coils for buds.

Assemble:
1. Arrange and glue the quilled shapes in the middle of the 6-1/2" square pink panel.
2. Frame that panel with the blue paper panel.
3. Brush the watercolors on the flowers and leaves. Let dry.
4. Add rhinestones to the flower centers and buds with white glue. Use the photo as a guide for placement.
5. Place the plastic bubble over the quilled arrangement and mount in the back of the journal window.
6. Frame the opening by taping the pink and dusty purple panels on top.
7. Tie the ribbon into a bow on the metal coil. ❏

Flowery Greetings
gift tags

The layered quilled shapes on these tags form three-dimensional designs. The flowers would look equally nice on cards or as accents on scrapbook pages.

Tulip Tags

SUPPLIES

Paper:

Light green vellum

Vellum sticker tags, 3-1/2" x 2"

Quilling paper strips, 1/8" wide –
  Green, red (or any other tulip
  flower color)

Quilling paper strips, 3/8" wide –
  Green

Tools & Other Supplies:

Basic tools and supplies for quilling
  and shaping (See the beginning of
  this section.)

Decorative edge scissors – Deckle,
  mini scallop

Dark green rick-rack

Scissors

INSTRUCTIONS

Make the Quilled Shapes:

The different lengths create a selection of flower and leaf sizes.

1. Flowers and Buds (make 5 shapes per flower) – Cut 4" of red paper strips. Shape into teardrops.

2. Stems (make 2) – Cut 1-1/2" to 2" green paper strips. Glue two strips together to form a thicker stem. Curl with scissors for a slight curve.

3. Leaves (make 2 per stem) – Cut 3/8" green paper strips into 1-1/2" to 2" lengths. Cut each piece into a sword-shaped leaf. Curl with scissors to shape.

Assemble:

1. Glue three red teardrop shapes together to form the flower. Add a single shape on top to create the three-dimensional effect.

2. Place the tag sticker on the green vellum. Trim with decorative edge scissors.

3. Glue the flower to the tag. Add the stem and bud. Let dry.

4. Add the leaves, gluing them in place at the top and bottom of the leaf shape.

5. Cut an 8" piece of rickrack. Loop through the hole in the tag for a tie. ❏

Hollyhock Tags

SUPPLIES

Papers:

Light green vellum

Vellum sticker tags, 3-1/2" x 2"

Quilling paper strips, 1/8" wide – Blue, purple, yellow, light blue, light purple, light green

Tools & Other Supplies:

Basic tools and supplies for quilling and shaping (See the beginning of this section.)

Decorative edge scissors – Deckle, mini scallop

Yellow green rick-rack

INSTRUCTIONS

Make the Quilled Shapes:

The different lengths create a selection of flower and leaf sizes.

1. Flowers (make 6 to 7 per stalk) – Cut 2" yellow paper strips and glue to 4" or 5" blue or purple paper strips. Shape into multicolored loose coils.

2. Buds (make 3 to 4 per stalk) – Cut 2" to 3" of light blue or light purple paper strips. Shape into tight coils.

3. Leaves (make 9 to 10 per stalk) – Cut 3" to 4" light green paper strips. Shape into teardrops.

Assemble:

1. Glue five flowers together in a staggered line with the buds at the top. Glue the leaves clustered around the flowers.

2. Glue two flowers on top at the base to create the three-dimensional effect.

3. Place the tag sticker on the green vellum. Trim with decorative edge scissors.

4. Glue the arrangement of quilled shapes to the tags.

5. Cut an 8" piece of rickrack. Loop through the hole in the tag for a tie. ❏

Paper Tole

In paper tole, cutout motifs of an identical image are shaped, layered, and glued to a base. Using an uplifting adhesive for gluing creates a dimensional effect. Some common names given to this art form include three-dimensional paper tole, dimensional paper tole, three-dimensional art, three-dimensional decoupage, and dimensional art, to name a few. All refer to the same basic craft.

The word *tole* is thought to have come from the French word for the craft of beating metal into a raised shape. Paper tole is thought to be an extension of decoupage and probably appeared in Europe after decoupage became popular in the 18th century. New paper designs and laser cut images make creating paper tole easier and faster. You can also use stickers, rubber stamps, scrapbook papers, and greeting cards as well as paper tole prints to make paper tole projects.

Supplies for Paper Tole

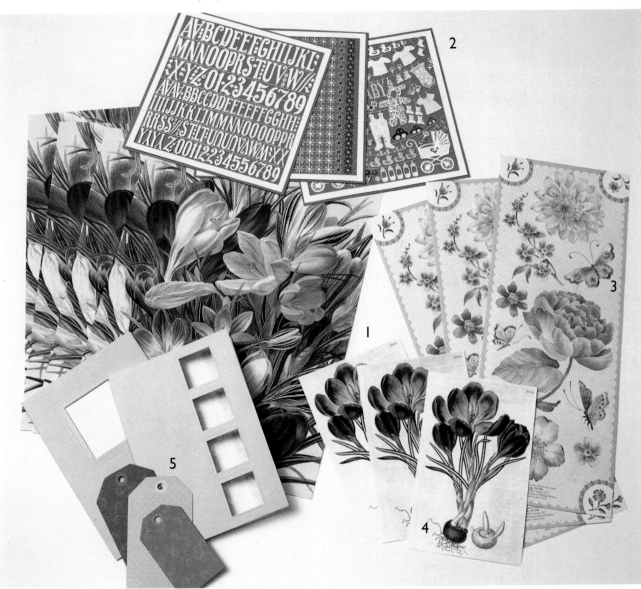

Paper Images for Paper Tole: 1) Scrapbook papers; 2) Laser cut motifs; 3) Stickers; 4) Greeting cards; 5) Card and tag blanks

Base

Paper tole designs are usually created on a **canvas board or other stiff backing board** and framed as wall decorations. You can also make unique table ornaments, greeting cards, and box decorations with paper tole designs. I have included designs for wooden frames and instructions for using a polymer coating on paper tole for a beautiful, professional finish that is both practical and attractive.

Paper Images

Papers with large individual motifs work best. There are many possibilities, including multiple paper prints, greeting cards, decorative scrapbook paper, paper tole prints, stamped images, or color-photocopied photographs.

Continued on next page

Supplies for Paper Tole, continued

Scrapbook Papers: Decorative scrapbook papers come in a huge assortment of colors, designs, and textures. In just one walk around a scrapbooking, crafts, or art supply store you will discover many papers that will inspire you. Choose the heavier card-weight papers for the best results, and look for matching printed verses and stickers to embellish your projects.

Laser Cuts: These delicate images have laser cut intricate details and are ready to snip from their frames and layer on a base. The finely detailed designs come in colors or white, ready for custom tinting with chalks, inkpads, or acrylic paints. Laser cuts are shaped before they are adhered to the base with glue dots.

Stickers: A huge selection of designs and motifs is available as stickers. Purchasing multiple packages of the same motifs provides instant paper tole design elements. The motifs come cut and attached to a backing paper, ready to peel off. You simply stick them on card-weight paper, cut out, shape, and layer.

Stamped Images: Rubber stamps offer an economical way to make multiple images for paper tole. The wide selection of motifs available offers many possibilities for designing paper tole images.

Cutting & Shaping Tools

The success of paper tole pieces is greatly dependent on the cutting and shaping of the cut piece.

Art Knife: An art knife is generally used for cutting out the inside areas of motifs. For most cutting jobs, a round handled knife with #11 blade works best. For successful cutting, always use a new blade, and always work on a **self-healing cutting mat.** (It prevents you from marring your work surface.)

Scissors: A sharp pair of *small, pointed scissors* is used for intricate and precise cutting of motifs. For snipping laser cuts, *tweezer scissors* make the intricate cutting quick and easy.

Shaping Tools: After the motifs are cut out, they are ready to be shaped. This shaping is important for the overall dimensional effect. Use a **nylon shaping tool** or a **large embossing tool** on a soft surface, such as a **thin foam mat.**

Tweezers

A good pair of sharp *pointed tweezers* is handy for placing small cutouts. Tweezers are especially useful when working with small delicate laser cut pieces and tiny glue dots.

Adhesives

Dimensional adhesives are used for mounting and elevating the cut and shaped pieces on the base. You will also need non-dimensional adhesives.

Glue Dots: Glue dots are used when gluing cut pieces to a paper base such as a card or scrapbook page and for gluing laser cuts. Glue dots come in a variety of sizes, from very tiny (1/8") to larger (1/2") sizes in both round and square shapes.

Some glue dots are pieces of foam with adhesive on both sides; others are dimensional clear dots of glue on a protective paper roll.

Glue gun: A glue gun with clear glue sticks is a great way to provide instant dimensional lift to a cutout and gives sturdy and strong support on items such as box tops. You have to work quickly, however, and you rarely have a chance to adjust the image if it's in the wrong place.

Clear Silicone Glue: Silicone glue is the traditional adhesive for paper tole. It dries slowly, allowing you to re-adjust the images and providing sturdy support. It can be messy, so using a toothpick to apply a small amount of glue to the backs of small pieces is recommended. Be sure to purchase silicone glue made for paper.

Glaze Coating

To enhance the three-dimensional effects, many paper tole artists like to apply a glaze coat to the image. Glaze coating is an option.

Decoupage Medium: Decoupage medium comes in a variety of finishes, including gloss, satin, matte, sepia-toned, and pearl. It is brushed on the cut and shaped paper pieces after they are mounted on the base or brushed on the images before cutting.

Polymer Coating: Polymer (liquid plastic) coating can be poured on a variety of surfaces and cures to provide a thick, permanent, waterproof, high gloss surface. For information about supplies and general instructions for using the coating, see "Basic Steps for Applying a Polymer Coating."

Pictured at right – Paper Tole Tools & Adhesives: 1) Art knife; 2) Cutting mat; 3) Scissors; 4) Tweezer scissors; 5) Shaping tools; 6) Tweezers; 7) Foam dots; 8) Glue gun; 9) Silicone glue; 10) Decoupage medium; 11) Ruler; 12) Embossing mat; 13) Craft glue; 14: Rubber stamps

Painting Techniques

Basecoating

This basecoating technique for wood surfaces ensures a smooth, plain painted finish that provides a trouble-free base for decorative and finishing techniques. Here's how:

1. To prepare the surface for painting, remove any hardware such as latches and hinges.
2. If your wooden surface has knots or dark patches, seal them with an acrylic sealer. Let the sealant dry completely before proceeding.
3. Apply the first coat of acrylic color with a large basecoating brush, evenly coating the surface with paint. Let dry completely before proceeding.
4. Sand the painted surface well with a medium (100 grit) sandpaper. (This results in a very smooth surface. Moisture in the acrylic paint tends to make the wood fibers stand up even if you sand well before the first coat.) Wipe or vacuum away the sanding dust.
5. Add another coat of paint on top of first. Let dry.
6. If needed, add a third coat of paint to cover the surface evenly. There should be no patches or visible brush marks. ❏

Distressing

This technique, which involves applying wax under or between layers of paint, instantly creates the look of old painted wood that has developed an interesting patina. You can apply one color of paint for a simple distressed finish, or use up to three different colors of paint for a layered vintage look. Sanding will reveal the layers of paint and the wood surface underneath. The piece look like it has naturally weathered with time. Here's how:

1. Rub a piece of uncolored wax (an old candle works well) on the wood surface in areas where the wood would normally show wear, such as the edges. (The wax will work as a resist and make sanding off the paint easier.)

2. Brush a single coat of paint over the wood, including the waxed areas. Let dry.
3. If you want to add a second color, rub more wax over the first layer of paint, then add a second coat of paint in another color.
4. To add more paint colors, continue layering wax and paint.
5. Apply the final coat of paint and let dry.
6. Sand the entire piece. Paint will come off easily in areas that were coated with wax. Wipe away the dust. ❏

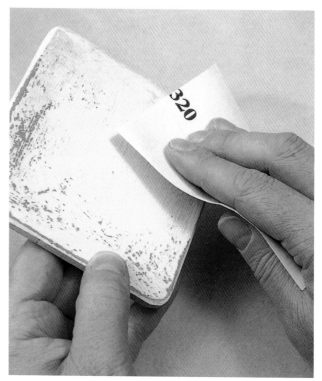

Sanding to reveal the wood underneath the paint, creating a distressed finish.

Texture Paint

Texture paint is another interesting option for surfaces. When dry, texture paint can be painted. It looks especially nice with a color wash. Here's how:

Option #1. Apply the texture paint to the surface with a palette knife, smoothing it to an even thickness. Texture paint dries slowly, allowing you ample working time. Allow to dry overnight to a hard finish, then paint as desired. ❑

Option #2: Use a stencil to apply the texture paint in a design. Position the stencil on the surface. Use a palette knife to apply the texture paint through the openings of the stencil. Lift off the stencil carefully to avoid smearing and let dry completely. ❑

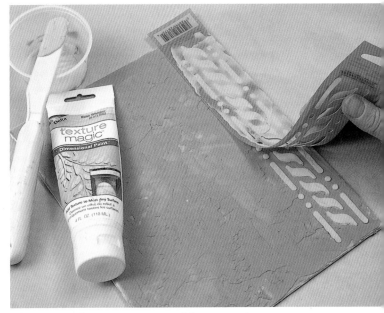

Using a stencil to create a pattern with texture paint.

Pictured below: Floral Images Framed Pictures. Instructions are found on page 110.

Paper Tole Technique

Paper tole involves layering elements cut from identical images. The first step is to choose your image and determine the different layers by identifying the background, middle ground, and foreground elements. With this information, you can now decide how many copies of the image you need. Intricate designs with a lot of depth can require many layers; simple images need only a few.

The background is usually the entire image. You build up the design using this image as your guide. Depth is created by shaping the middle ground and foreground elements before gluing them. TIP: For more detailed projects, use a system for organizing the cutouts that allows to you place the cut elements in order for easy positioning.

Basic Supplies for Paper Tole

Multiple paper images

Non-dimensional adhesive, such as a glue stick or decoupage medium

Scissors

Tweezers

Shaping tool and pad, such as a foam mat

Dimensional adhesive

Optional: Glaze coating

Basic Instructions

1. Adhere the background image to the base with decoupage medium or a glue stick.
2. Cut out the middle ground and foreground design elements from the duplicate images.
3. Shape the cutout images by placing the cut image face down on the foam mat. Rub and stretch the paper with a shaping tool to stretch and curve it.
4. Attach the pieces in place on the background image, using your chosen dimensional adhesive. Start with the larger middle ground pieces and work towards the smaller foreground pieces.
5. *Option:* Finish the dimensional image with a glaze coating. ❏

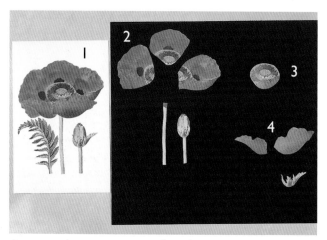

Images used to create a paper tole project:
1. Original image (the background)
2. Middle ground cut pieces, to apply on top of the background
3. Additional middle ground cut pieces, for applying next
4. Foreground cut pieces, for creating the final layers

After the cutout pieces have been shaped on a mat, adhesive was applied to the pieces one at a time and placed in position on the background with tweezers.

Stamped Paper Tole

You can create duplicate images easily with rubber stamps. Simply use the stamps to create a base image, then stamp the image(s) on card paper, color them, and cut them out. Add the cut layers with foam dots or another dimensional adhesive. Use permanent ink for stamping so the stamped images will not bleed when color is applied.

Basic Supplies

Rubber stamps (Simple motifs without a lot of edge details work best.)

Inkpad with permanent ink

Felt-tip markers, watercolors, or chalks in the colors of your choice

Scissors

Shaping tool and foam mat

Optional: Metallic paste

Basic Instructions

1. Using the permanent inkpad, stamp the image on the base, then on a separate piece of card paper three or more times.
2. Using felt markers, a thin wash of watercolors, or chalks, color the stamped images.
3. Cut out the colored stamped images. *Option:* Add highlights with metallic paste.
4. Working on a foam mat, use a shaping tool to shape the stamped images.
5. If needed, touch up the edges of the cut pieces to mask any white cut marks.
6. Adhere the cutouts to the base, following the instructions for the Paper Tole Technique.

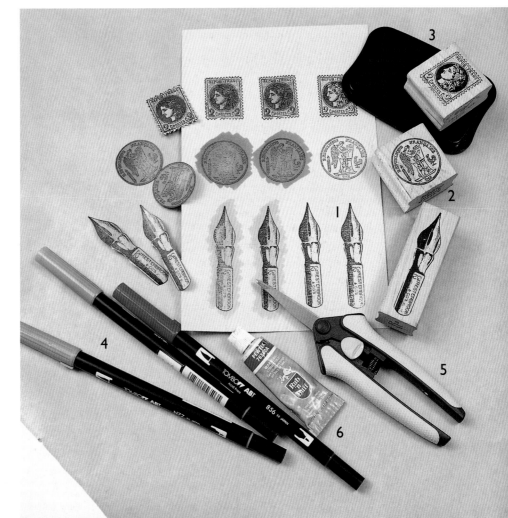

Supplies and Design Examples for Stamped Paper Tole: 1) Stamped images, colored and cut out; 2) Rubber stamps; 3) Inkpad with permanent ink; 4) Colored felt-tip markers; 5) Scissors; 6) Metallic paste

B Is for Baby
wall piece

This simple wall piece uses layered canvas boards and laser cut pieces. The result is a quick, easy, and charming paper tole project. The embossed effect on the large letter and canvas is achieved by painting laser cut images after gluing them in place. Applying a glossy varnish coating highlights this effect.

SUPPLIES

Base:

Stretched canvas, 8" square, 5/8" thick

Stretched canvas, 5" square, 1-1/2" thick

Wooden letter "B", 4" tall (Baby's initial could also be used.)

Papers:

Laser cut motif sheets – 2 sheets baby theme, 1 sheet mini daisy

Embellishments:

2 wooden peg-type clothespins

Green satin ribbon, 1" wide

Teddy bear, 2"

22 gauge purple wire

Blue button

Tools & Other Supplies:

Basic paper tole supplies (See the beginning of this section.)

Acrylic paints – Soft muted green, blue, light lavender

Glue dots or silicone glue

Decoupage medium, gloss

White craft glue

Paint brushes

2 small finishing nails

Hammer

INSTRUCTIONS

Paint:

1. Paint the top of the letter with blue, the inside edges with green, and the outside edges with purple.
2. Paint the top of the small canvas with green. Paint two opposite sides blue. Paint the other two sides purple.
3. Paint the top of the large canvas with blue. Paint two opposite sides purple. Paint the other two sides green.
4. Paint one clothes peg green. Paint the other blue. Let dry.

Glue:

1. Glue the base pieces (the large canvas, small canvas, and letter) together, using the photo as a guide for placement. Use craft glue and weigh down the pieces while they dry for a strong bond.
2. On the top of the small canvas, cut and glue the laser cut images of baby items.
3. On the top of the letter, cut and glue small daisies.
4. Apply an additional coat of paint to both surfaces to create the embossed effect.
5. Cut out the baby clothes and glue them flat on the large canvas with the decoupage medium. Use the top connecting paper strip for the clothesline. See the project photo for placement ideas.
6. Cut and shape another set of baby clothes. Shape the paper pieces so it seems that they are blowing in a gentle breeze.
7. Glue the shaped cutouts in place with dimensional glue.
8. Glue the teddy and the clothes pegs to the sides of the base canvas with white glue. TIP: Use two small nails to secure clothes pegs to the canvas.

Finish:

1. Shape the wire into a clothes hanger.
2. Cut out letters to spell BABY. Shape the letters and glue them to the clothes hanger, using white glue. Place the clothes hanger in the teddy's hand.
3. To create the wall hanger, tie the green ribbon to the top of one clothes peg. Allow enough for hanging, then tie the end of the ribbon to the other clothes peg, ending with a bow.
4. Glue a small button to the bow. ❑

Welcome to Toyland
baby cards & tags

These two cards and three tags are made with same papers as the wall piece pictured on the previous page. The elements were snipped from the sheets and glued with tiny drops of white glue. Glue dots are used for dimension; rhinestones and decorative fibers are used as accents.

Toyland Card

SUPPLIES

Base:
White card with four windows

Papers:
Laser cut motif sheets – 2 sheets
    baby theme
Blue dotted

Tools & Other Supplies:
Basic paper tole supplies (See the
    beginning of this section.)
Glue dots
White craft glue

INSTRUCTIONS

1. Cut the dotted paper to fit inside the card.
2. Choose toy motifs from the laser cut sheets – two of the same motif for each window.
3. Affix one motif in each window with tiny dots of white craft glue. Glue a second set over the first, using glue dots for dimension.
4. Spell TOYLAND! with laser cut letters. Glue to the card front with white craft glue. ❏

Baby Carriage Card

SUPPLIES

Base:
White card with one window

Papers:
Laser cut motif sheets – 2 sheets
    baby theme
Blue dotted

Tools & Other Supplies:
Basic paper tole supplies (See the
    beginning of this section.)
Glue dots
White craft glue

INSTRUCTIONS

1. Cut the dotted paper to fit inside the card.
2. Choose two carriage motifs from the laser cut sheets.
3. Affix one motif in the window with tiny dots of white craft glue. Glue a second over the first, using glue dots for dimension.
4. Frame the window with strips of colored print paper.
5. Glue a rattle motif at one corner. ❏

Baby Gift Tags

SUPPLIES

Base:
Blue dotted gift tags

Papers:
Laser cut motif sheets –
    2 sheets baby theme,
    1 sheet mini daisy

Tools & Other Supplies:
Basic paper tole supplies (See the
    beginning of this section.)
Glue dots
White craft glue
Decorative fibers
Self-adhesive colored stones
Optional: Wooden clothespin

INSTRUCTIONS

1. Using the project photo as a guide, decorate the tags with the various leftover bits and pieces of baby motifs, frames, letters, and daisies.
2. Add stones as accents.
3. Loop decorative fibers through the holes of the tags for attaching.
4. *Option:* Add a wooden clothespin as an accent. ❏

Miracle Monogram
desk accessory

Make this as a gift for an office buddy or to dress up your own desk. I chose the letter "M"
and the theme "miracle." What other letters and themes might you create?

SUPPLIES

Base:

Wooden letter M, 4" tall

Papers:

Laser cut motif sheets – 1 sheet
each mini colored daisy, large
white daisy, white alphabet

Small tag in a matching color

Tools & Other Supplies:

Basic paper tole supplies (See the
beginning of this section.)

Acrylic paint – Soft taupe

Sandpaper, 100 grit

20 gauge copper wire

Brown permanent pen

White craft glue

Dimensional adhesive (Glue dots *or*
glue gun and glue sticks)

Acrylic varnish, satin finish

Laser cut design sheets

INSTRUCTIONS

1. Basecoat the wooden letter with taupe paint. Let dry.

2. Sand the edges of the letter for a distressed look. Wipe away the dust.

3. Using white craft glue, attach colored mini daisies around the edge of the letter.

4. Cut out "MIRACLES HAPPEN" from the alphabet sheet. Glue flat to the letter.

5. Glue a few mini daises flat to the letter, using the photo as a guide for placement.

6. Write "I believe in miracles" on the paper tag with the brown marker.

7. Use a small piece of wire to attach the tag to the wooden letter.

8. Snip large daisies from design sheet. Attach to the letter using a dimensional adhesive. See the project photo for placement ideas.

9. Using the photo as a guide, add copper wire and twist decoratively to make a flower stem. Add daisy to the top end of the wire.

10. Coat everything with two coats satin varnish. Let dry. ❑

She Loves Me
card & tag

I used some of the leftover daisies from the large white daisy laser cut sheet I bought to make the project on the previous page to decorate a window card and a tag.

A complete daisy was placed in the top window of the card. In the other three windows, I placed daisies with successively fewer petals, and glued the petals I removed to the card front. I used a brown marker to write "she loves me!"

The tag has two layered daisies and some pieces of shimmery cords for attaching. ❏

Flowers & Dots
monogram card & tag

I used some of the leftovers of the mini colored daisy and white alphabet design sheets from the "Miracles Happen" project to make this card and tag – you don't need a lot of materials to make a big impact. I colored the edges of the letters with chalk and used glue dots to raise the letters for a three-dimensional effect.

Tiny drops of white glue were used to glue the daisy frame on the card and the heart-shaped daisy cluster on the tag. Self-adhesive stones decorate the centers of some daisies. Ribbon and shiny cord were looped through the hole in the tag. ❏

Vintage Symbolism
stamp box

This example of stamped paper tole uses hot glue as a dimensional adhesive, adding strength to the paper tole pieces. You can use it to store all sorts of things, including stamps.

SUPPLIES

Base:
Papier mache box, 4" cube

Papers:
Light beige card stock
Gray tile motif decorative paper
Brown suede paper

Embellishments:
Pewter stickers
3/4 yd. ribbon, 1/2" wide –
  Black with gold edging
Silver buckle

Tools & Other Supplies:
Basic paper tole supplies (See the
  beginning of this section.)
Acrylic paint – Warm gray
Permanent inkpad – Black
Felt markers in various colors
Glue stick
Glue gun and glue sticks
Rubber stamps – Script, coin,
  postage stamp, pen nib
Awl

INSTRUCTIONS

Prepare:
1. Basecoat the box inside and out with warm gray acrylic paint. Let dry.
2. With black ink, stamp the various images on the decorative paper.
3. Stamp multiple images of the coin, pen nib, and postage stamp on beige card stock. Color the multiple images with the felt markers.
4. Cut out the stone tiles from the decorative paper.

Assemble:
1. Glue the stone tile cutouts to the top and sides of the box. When gluing, place all the images below the lip of the lid.
2. Cut out the colored and stamped images.
3. Adhere the images flat to the box with a glue stick.
4. Add the pewter stickers.
5. Shape and adhere the cut images, using hot glue for dimension.
6. Using an awl, make a hole through the sticker on the top of the box for the ribbon. Cut a loop of ribbon and thread it through the hole. Glue the ends on the inside of the lid with hot glue.
7. Glue the ribbon and buckle around the edge of the lid.
8. Cut three 3-3/4" square panels from the suede paper. Use them to line the lid, the outside bottom of the box, and the inside bottom of the box. ❏

Wishes, Hopes & Dreams
card

This card is crafted using stickers for the paper tole design. Layering adds dimension and interest.

SUPPLIES

Base:

Black card – 5-1/2" square (folded size)

Papers:

3 pkgs. floral stickers

Decorative paper (to match sticker background)

Lightweight card – Black, light beige

Tag cut from decorative paper

Embellishments:

Resin word stickers

Copper brad

Seed beads

Tools & Other Supplies:

Basic paper tole supplies (See the beginning of this section.)

Glue stick

Glue dots

Pictured right: Floral Stickers

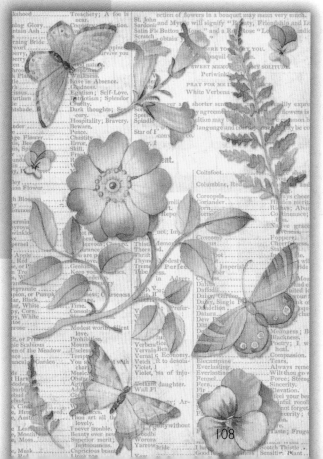

INSTRUCTIONS

See the project photo for placement ideas.

1. Cut a 5" square of decorative paper. Using a glue stick, glue it to the front of the card.
2. Cut strips of matching decorative paper 1/4" to 1/2" wide and 5-1/2" long. Glue to the card front.
3. Peel a flower motif and stick it on the card front. Peel two of the same flower motifs. Stick them on a piece of beige card paper.
4. Cut out the leaves and flower petals from the motifs adhered to the card paper. Shape them and adhere to the front of the card with glue dots to create the dimensional paper tole look.
5. Peel the butterfly and small pansy motifs and stick them on the card. Peel the same images and stick them on black card paper.
6. Cut out the butterfly and flower motifs from the card paper, leaving a very thin black border around the motifs. Shape them and adhere to the front of the card with glue dots.
7. Add clear resin word stickers to the front of the card.
8. Decorate the tag with a panel of decorative paper, stickers, and resin word stickers. Attach the tag to the card with the copper brad.
9. With white craft glue, add seed beads to the centers of the large flower motif and the pansy blossoms. ❏

Floral Images
framed pictures

These simple motifs are suitable for paper tole beginners. The textured backgrounds and textured frames visually link the pair. The flower images for these pictures were cut from note cards – an easy-to-use source of multiple images on strong, card-weight paper.

SUPPLIES

Base:

4 matching brushed gold frames – two 8" x 10", two 5" x 7"

2 canvas boards, 8" x 10"

Papers:

Images – 3 magnolia bud, 3 tulip blossom

Tissue paper with printed gold motifs

Tools & Other Supplies:

Basic paper tole supplies (See the beginning of this section.)

White craft glue

Glue gun and glue sticks *or* silicone glue

Acrylic varnish, gloss finish

Decoupage medium

Gold metallic paste

Texture paste

Palette knife

Border stencil, 1" wide floral motif

Dark brown acrylic gel

INSTRUCTIONS

Create the Frames:

1. Use the palette knife to spread a thin layer of texture paste over both canvas boards. Let dry.
2. Position the border stencil along the edges of the canvas boards and apply texture paste through the cutout motifs on the stencil. Gently lift and remove the stencil.
3. Stencil the sides of the boards with texture paste. Let dry. Stencil the tops and bottoms of the boards. Let dry.
4. Working one small section at a time, brush brown gel over the raised textures. Immediately wipe off the excess for an antique look. Let dry.
5. Tear the decorative tissue paper into pieces. Using decoupage medium, apply the pieces randomly to the canvas board. Let dry.
6. Highlight the textured canvas with metallic wax, rubbing the wax over the tissue paper and the textured designs.
7. Using the three copies of each image, create a paper tole flower design in the center of each canvas board. See the beginning of this section for detailed instructions. Use white craft glue for the first layer and a dimensional adhesive for the remaining pieces.
8. When the glue is dry, brush the flowers with gloss varnish. Let dry.
9. Mount one canvas board in each 8" x 10" frame.
10. Use white glue to glue a matching 5" x 7" frame – with or without the glass – to frame the flowers. Weight the frame with books while drying for a good bond. ❏

110

Garden Theme
bulletin board

This bulletin board frame – suitable for home or office – is made with scrapbook paper images and finished with a polymer coating. The basecoat color was chosen to match the background color of the scrapbook paper. This makes the cutting easier and the overall effect look more professional.

SUPPLIES

Base:
Wooden frame, 12" x 16"
Cork board to fit frame
Backing board to fit frame

Papers:
3 sheets floral scrapbook paper

Tools & Other Supplies:
Basic paper tole supplies (See the beginning of this section.)
Polymer coating supplies (See the beginning of the Collage section for a list.)
Clear varnish spray
Foam stamps – Lower case alphabet, 1" and 1-1/2"
Rubber stamps – Words (e.g., "color," "beauty," "wind") *or* small alphabet stamps
Green inkpad
Acrylic paint – Light green (or a color that matches background color of your scrapbook paper)
Fine permanent marker – Brown
Thin white glue
Glue gun and glue sticks
Flat clear marbles
Thumbtacks
Small sea sponge

INSTRUCTIONS

1. Basecoat the frame with green paint. Let dry.
2. Stamp the large words, using the foam alphabet stamps. (I choose "rain", "sun," "air," and "earth.")
3. Stamp the small words, using word stamps or making your own words with small alphabet stamps.
4. Sponge green acrylic paint over the words to lighten and fade parts of the stamped letters. Let dry.
5. Spray the frame with two coats of clear varnish. Seal coat both sides of the scrapbook paper with clear varnish spray. Let dry.
6. Cut out at least three copies of each image you want to use from the scrapbook paper. Leave one image of each motif whole and cut the others into pieces for paper tole.
7. Glue the whole images flat on the frame, using thin white glue.
8. Shape and attach the dimensional pieces in place with hot glue.
9. Add details (e.g., butterfly antennae, bee's legs) to the images with the brown marker.
10. Coat with the frame and paper tole images with polymer coating. See "Basic Steps for Applying a Polymer Coating" in the Collage section for instructions.
11. When the coating has cured, install the corkboard and backing in the frame.
12. Make matching pins for the bulletin board by gluing flat marbles over small images on the scrapbook paper with white glue. Let dry. Trim away the excess paper.
13. Glue each marble to a thumbtack. ❑

Fields of Flowers
framed mirror

Floral stickers were used to create the floral paper tole decorations for this wooden frame.
The distressed painted background incorporates stamped images.

SUPPLIES

Base:

Wooden frame with mirror,
 10" square

Papers:

3 sheets floral stickers

Lightweight beige card stock

Tools & Other Supplies:

Basic paper tole supplies (See the
 beginning of this section.)

Acrylic paints – Gray green, yellow
 ocher

White wax candle stub

100 grit sandpaper

Rubber stamps – Script swirl,
 words

Blue inkpad

Acrylic varnish – Matte finish

Hanger

Paint brushes

Glue gun and glue sticks

INSTRUCTIONS

1. Basecoat the frame with gray green acrylic paint. Let dry.
2. Rub some areas of the frame with wax.
3. Coat the frame with yellow ocher paint. Let dry.
4. Sand the paint to create the distressed old painted look. Wipe away the dust.
5. Stamp the images randomly on the frame with blue ink.
6. Sand again, lightly, to fade the stamped images and further distress the frame.
7. Coat the frame with the matte varnish. Let dry.
8. Peel and stick the floral images on the frame, using the photo as a guide. Overlap the mirror and edges of frame slightly and trim away the excess.
9. Peel the same floral images and stick on lightweight beige card stock. Cut out the elements.
10. Shape the pieces to create dimension.
11. Attach the dimensional pieces with hot glue.
12. Brush the paper images with a coat of acrylic varnish to strengthen and protect the paper tole. Let dry.
13. Attach a hanger to the back of the frame. ❑

Pictured below: floral stickers

Washi Chigiri-e

Washi chigiri-e is an ancient Japanese art form that uses torn paper to create the look of paintings. Paper crafts have a long tradition in Japan. Techniques for making pictures by pasting paper on a base include "hari-e" (pasted pictures), "chigiri-e" (torn pictures), and "kiri-e" (cut pictures.)

The term washi refers to any Japanese paper ("wa" meaning "Japan," "shi" meaning "paper.") The washi used for chigiri is Japanese unryu. This "cloud-dragon paper" is named for the long floating strands of kozo fibers, which give it beauty and strength. These papers are sometimes called rice paper, but that's not correct – Asian paper is not made from a rice pulp base, although rice straw is sometimes added for texture.

To make the chigiri-e images, the artist tears washi paper of various color combinations and weights and glues them to a background to make what appears to be a watercolor, a pastel, or an oil painting. Shikishi is the name of the board that forms the base for chigiri-e.

Chigiri-e is also described as fine pictures "painted" with paper or "washi collage." The word "chigiri-e" is a combination of two basic Japanese words. "Chigiri" is the noun form of the verb "chigiru," which means "to tear," and "-e" is an artwork or picture painted with the tearing of washi paper. Traditional subjects are flowers and oriental landscapes. The layering of the washi, whether torn or cut, creates the look of watercolors with the texture of an oil painting.

Cherry Blossoms Plate & Card. Instructions begin on page 140.

Basic Supplies

Washi Paper

All papers used for chigiri-e include long fibers that give them strength. You can buy pre-colored paper or uncolored paper.

Pre-colored washi paper comes with multiple shades of colors on each sheet that gradually blend into each other. It's ready to be torn and glued.

Plain, uncolored washi paper comes in a wide variety of weights, from tissue thin to thick and heavy. I prefer uncolored paper. After I cut or tear the paper shapes, I color the pieces with acrylic or watercolor paints. The sizing in the heavier papers affects how the paper absorbs paint.

Waterbrush

A **waterbrush** is a combination brush and water container. Water is added to the handle, allowing a continuous, even flow of water from the bristles. You use the waterbrush to make the shapes you want to make before tearing.

Option: You can also use a #4 round paint brush and clean water to trace the shapes on the paper before tearing.

Paints & Brushes

I generally use **tube acrylic paints** to color the paper shapes. Since the paints are diluted quite a bit, using good quality paints is important.

I also love **shimmering watercolors** that impart a beautiful glimmer to the finished project.

I apply the paints with soft, good quality **flat watercolor or acrylic brushes** in a variety of sizes (1/4" to 1").

Adhesives

Glue Stick – A glue stick can be used to adhere the finished paper pieces to a paper surface such as a card or in a journal. When working with a glue stick, have some gluing sheets (wax paper, deli sheets, or pages from an old phone book) to keep the fronts of your images free of excess glue.

Nori Paste – Nori means "paste" in Japanese. It is the recommended glue for delicate washi papers. This rice paste dries clear and does not wrinkle or soak through delicate papers. It dries slowly so you can make changes. When dry, it offers a strong, waterproof bond. Nori paste can be used on paper or wooden surfaces.

Decoupage Medium – Regular podge-type decoupage mediums or thin-bodied white glue can be used to attach paper pieces to prepared wooden, glass, or metal surfaces. Decoupage mediums come in a variety of finishes, including gloss, satin, matte, sepia-toned, and pearl.

Miscellaneous Tools & Supplies

Wax Paper protects your work surface and provides a foundation for coloring the paper shapes. You also could use **freezer paper**.

Water-erase Transfer Paper is handy for transferring shapes onto heavier, opaque washi paper. The light blue marks from the transfer paper disappear when water is added. To use, place the washi paper, the transfer paper (face down), and the pattern on your work surface. (TIP: Test to make sure the transfer paper is face down by making a mark.) Trace over the design with a pen, then cut or tear the shapes along the pattern marks.

Palette – A plastic palette is handy for mixing and diluting the paints with water. You could also use a sheet of **wax paper** for a palette.

Spray Bottle – Use a spray bottle to apply a fine mist of water to the paper shapes before adding the colors. This allows the paint to gently blend into the paper for stress-free and easy shading.

Chigiri-e Supplies: 1) Washi papers – Pre-colored, translucent unryu and opaque washi paper; 2) Waterbrush; 3) Wax paper; 4) Water-erase transfer paper; 5) Tube paints; 6) Sparkling watercolors; 7) Brushes – #4 round, 1/4" flat, 1/2" flat; 8) Palette; 9) Glue stick; 10) Nori paste

The Basic Chigiri-e Technique

Follow these steps to create a torn paper (chigiri-e) project. The example is an abstract floral design. All the projects in this section have a loose composition that allows for variations.

1. Tear

Tear the pattern pieces from washi paper. Do not worry if your pieces vary from the pattern; the composition looks better with a variety of sizes and shapes. Different papers tear differently, creating various kinds of torn edges – this makes your finished piece unique. TIP: Tear extra pieces so you have a nice variety to work with as you create your composition.

When tearing thin, transparent washi:
Place a piece of wax paper over the pattern, then the washi paper. (The pattern will be visible.) Using a waterbrush or a clean paint brush and water, trace the pattern lines with a thin stream of water. Carefully tear the paper shapes along the wet outlines (Photo 1) and place the pieces on a piece of wax paper. TIP: Good lighting makes it easier to see the wet outlines.

When using thicker, opaque washi:
Use water-erase transfer paper to transfer the pattern lines. Tear the pattern pieces and place on wax paper. The marks from the transfer paper will disappear when the pieces are moistened with water. Moisten the outlines with a waterbrush before tearing.

Creating thin stems:
Thin stems can be cut, torn, or twisted, which is the traditional method. To twist a stem, tear a strip 1" wide and the length of the pattern piece. Wet the strip with clean water and twirl between your fingers to form a long thin strand. (Photo 2) Place on wax paper.

2. Prepare to Paint

When all pattern pieces are torn or cut out and placed on wax paper, they are ready to color. Sort the pattern pieces on the wax paper according to the colors they will be painted, for example, place all the green leaves together, all the pink petals together, etc. Make sure none of the pieces are touching.

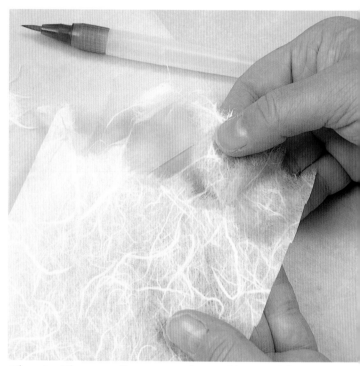

Photo 1 – The pattern lines are traced on washi paper with a waterbrush. The pieces are torn from the paper.

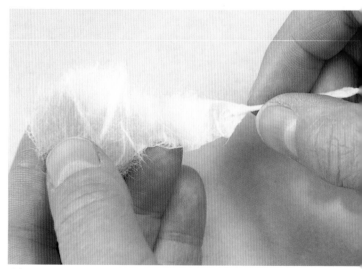

Photo 2 – Twisting a stem.

If you are using tube acrylics, place a small amount of each paint color on your palette. *If you are using shimmering watercolors,* mist the tops of the paint containers to moisten the paint.

Mist the paper pieces with clean water so they are well dampened. Thicker papers with more sizing will need a lot more water and time for the paper to absorb it. Do not over-mist – this creates puddles between the pieces. If needed, soak up excess water with a folded paper towel before adding the color.

Photo 3 – Coloring the pieces with sparkling watercolors.

3. Paint the Pieces

Dip the paint brush in the color and dilute the paint on the palette – it should be the consistency of ink. Touch the color to the edge of the piece, letting the color bleed into the shape. (Photo 3) Color one side of the paper, leaving the other side white.

- Very little color is needed; the color will be lighter when it dries.
- The entire piece does not need to be colored. Leave unpainted areas for a lovely shaded effect.
- Add more paint to intensify the color.
- Colors can be layered. Project instructions include suggestions for mixing and applying colors.

Let the pieces dry completely. The pieces are fragile when wet – don't try to move them until they are dry. You can dry them quickly with a hair dryer, but be careful. When completely dry, they can suddenly blow off the wax paper.

4. Glue

Glue the pieces to the surface. Use the recommended glue to attach the paper shapes to the base. (Photo 4)

5. *Option:* Add a Finish Coat

Projects on paper do not require a finish, but surfaces such as trays will need protection. Acrylic varnish or a polymer coating works best. Refer to the Collage section for more detailed information.

Photo 4 – Pasting pieces in place with nori paste.

Washi Kiri-e Technique Variation

The kiri-e technique is done the same way as chigiri-e with one main difference – the shapes are cut rather than torn from washi paper. Because the paper used is thin, it is easy to cut six to eight shapes at a time.

Here's how:
1. Fold the washi.
2. Transfer the shape to the top fold with water-erase transfer paper.
3. Cut out the shape with sharp scissors.
4. Follow the steps for the Basic Chigiri-e Technique to color and glue the shapes to create the project.

Pacific Northwest Trio
wall grouping

This project is a great example of combining the kiri-e and chigiri-e techniques to create an interesting composition. I used photographs of beaches near my home in the Pacific Northwest for inspiration. The small canvas is a close-up of the tide and rocks, the medium canvas is the beach, and the large canvas is the whole landscape.

The contrast of torn paper edges for the waves and islands and cut paper edges of the rocks and horizon give the arrangements interest and the look of a watercolor painting. Vary the number of elements and placements to suit your own arrangement.

SUPPLIES

Base:

3 stretched canvas boards, 7-1/2" square, 8" x 10", 12" square

Washi Paper:

White unryu

Tools & Other Supplies:

Decoupage medium, matte finish

Paint brushes

Sponge brush

Tube acrylic paints – Sky blue, ultramarine blue, Payne's gray, light brown, dark brown, yellow oxide

Old toothbrush (for spattering)

Basic supplies for washi chigiri-e (See the beginning of this section.)

Pictured right: The photo that inspired this project.

INSTRUCTIONS

1. Tear and cut the pieces using the example for the patterns and the project photo of the finished project for ideas. Make the pieces for the large wave and beach 2" longer than the width of the canvas so they can be wrapped over the edges.
2. Using the color palette, color the paper pieces for the small and medium canvases.

Continued on page 124

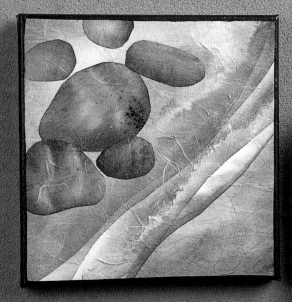

Pacific Northwest Trio
Pictured on page 123

Continued from page 122

Rocks – Browns, gray, and yellow. Let dry. Use an old toothbrush to spatter dark gray spots on parts of some rocks.

Beach – Light brown and gray.

Water – Blues and a small touch of gray.

3. Using the color palette, color the paper pieces for the large canvas.

Sky – Gray and ultramarine blue.

Islands – Gray and ultramarine blue. The islands in the foreground are darker; the islands in the background are a lighter shade.

Water – Sky blue and a small touch of gray. Let dry.

4. Position the shapes on the canvas and adhere with decoupage medium. Wrap the paper over the edges of the canvases to cover them.

5. Brush with two coats of decoupage medium, letting each coat dry completely.

6. Paint the edges of the canvas with undiluted Payne's gray. *Option:* Use a sponge brush (as I did) to paint a very narrow border on front of each canvas. With a sponge brush, you can paint a straight edge without using masking tape. ❏

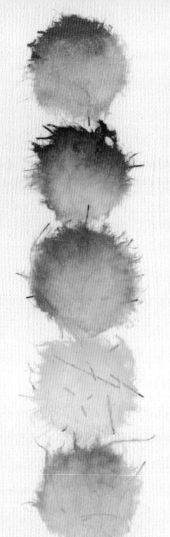

Golden Vineyard
tray

Both chigiri-e and kiri-e shapes decorate a plain wooden tray. The clean edges of the cut grape shapes complement the torn edges of the leaves. My grapes are golden in color; for a different look, use burgundy or purple to color your grapes.

I used a piece of decorative paper for the weathered background, but you could paint the background instead. Follow the "Distressing" instructions in the Paper Tole section.

Pictured on pages 126-127.

Golden Vineyard

SUPPLIES

Base:

Wooden tray, 10" x 13"

4 wooden knobs, 1"

Papers:

Decorative paper with white
    crackled paint look, 12" x 9"

Washi paper – White unryu

Tools & Other Supplies:

Acrylic paints for tray – Black,
    yellow ocher

Decoupage medium, satin finish

Paint brushes

Tube acrylic paints – Brown, deep
    yellow, metallic copper, lime
    green, olive green, sap green

Gold metallic paste

Black jute

Label holder

White craft glue

4 small screws, 3/4"

Screwdriver

Hammer

Basic supplies for washi chigiri-e
    and kiri-e (See the beginning of
    this section.)

INSTRUCTIONS

Prepare the Tray:

1. Use white craft glue to attach the
   wooden knobs to the bottom of
   the tray for the feet. For a more
   secure hold, install small screws
   through the corners of the tray.

2. Basecoat the inside of the tray
   with the yellow ocher. Basecoat
   sides and the bottom with
   black. Let dry.

3. Rub gold metallic paste over the
   top edge of the tray and the feet.

4. Use decoupage medium to adhere
   the decorative paper to the inside
   bottom surface of the tray.

5. Paint an irregular border with
   yellow ocher to conceal the cut
   edges of the paper.

Create the Design:

1. Cut the grape shapes from washi
   paper.

2. Tear the leaf shapes.

3. Make the stems by twisting various lengths of washi strips.

4. Place all the pieces on wax
   paper. Using tube acrylic paints,
   color the pieces, using the photo
   as a guide.
   Grapes – Yellow, lime green
   with small touches of brown.
   Color only one side of each
   grape, leaving white highlights.
   Leaves – Greens at the edges, with
   touches of copper in the centers.
   Stems – Brown and copper.
   Let dry.

5. Position the shapes and adhere
   using decoupage medium. Refer
   to the photo for placement ideas.
   Try overlapping the elements as
   well as placing them on the sides
   of the tray. (The placement is
   loose; change it to accommo-
   date your artistic ideas.)

6. Wrap black jute around the
   handle openings. Glue the ends
   to secure.

7. Nail a label holder to the front.
   Add a label with the grape variety
   name. ❏

Autumn Landscape
coat rack

All the paper shapes that create this serene landscape were torn. The design is highlighted with stamped words. The design is very loose – feel free to change the number of elements and their placement to suit your own design ideas.

SUPPLIES

Base:
Wooden board with pegs, 19" x 8"

Washi Paper:
Japan Ogura, jute fibers (heavier, light tan colored paper with golden fibers)

Tools & Other Supplies:
Tube acrylic paints – Metallic copper, yellow oxide, yellow deep, Indian red oxide, olive green, raw umber, brown madder

Decoupage medium, matte finish

Paint brushes

Sponge brush

Rubber stamps – Lower case alphabets, 1" and 1-1/2" tall; uppercase alphabet, 1/2" tall

Inkpads – Brown permanent ink, gold ink

Basic supplies for washi chigiri-e (See the beginning of this section.)

INSTRUCTIONS

1. Remove the pegs from the board.
2. Tear the pieces, using the example for the patterns and the project photo for ideas. Make the pieces 2" longer than the width of the board so they can overlap the edges.

Continued on page 130

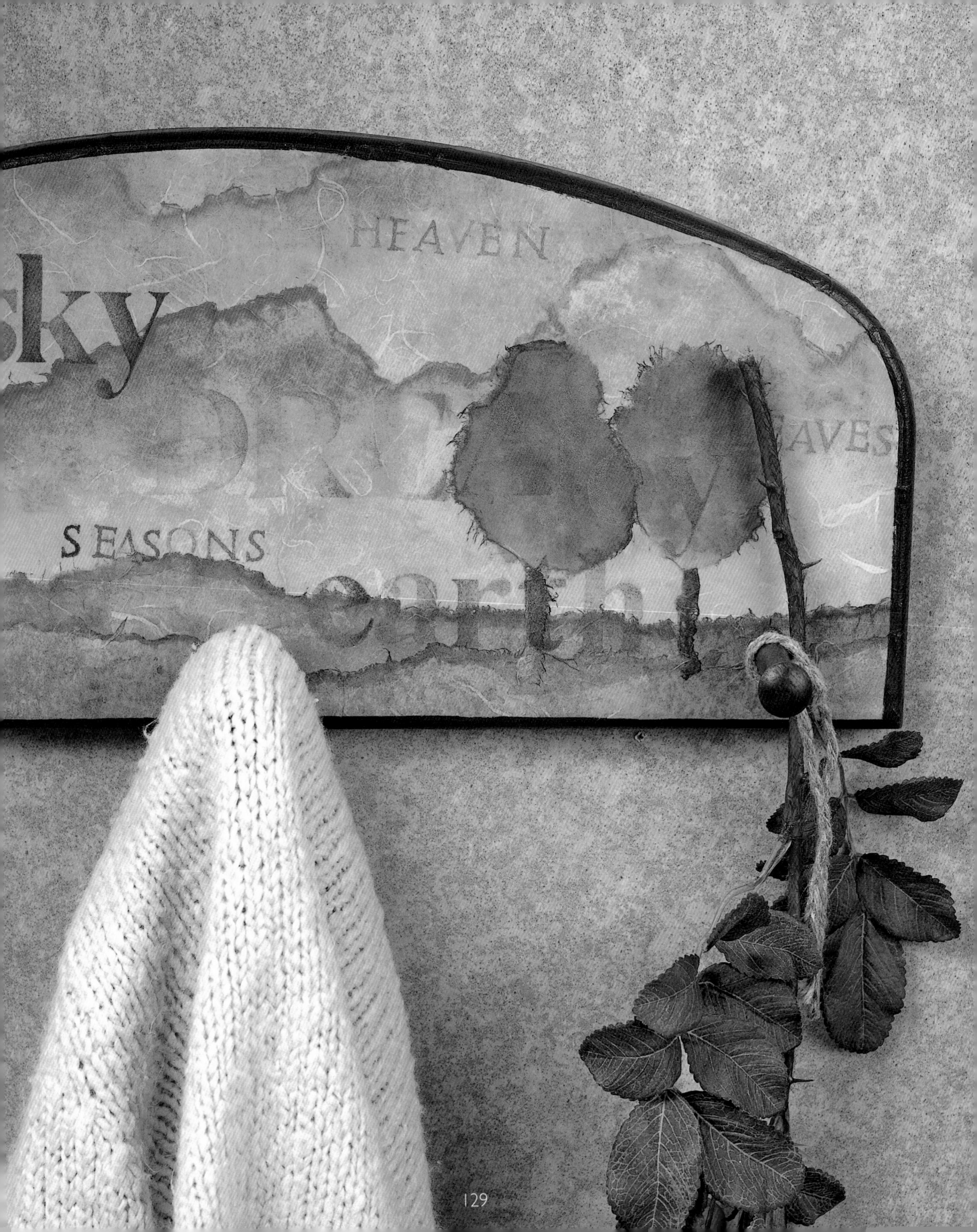
HEAVEN
sky
SEASONS
earth

Autumn Landscape

continued from page 128

3. Using tube acrylics, color the pieces:
   Sky – Reds, yellows, and copper. The top edges are red tones and gradually blend into the yellow shades at the bottom. Adding copper gives the colors a slight metallic tinge.
   Ground – Blend the greens, browns, and copper.
   Trees – Blend the greens, browns, and copper with tiny touches of red. Paint the tree trunks with raw umber. Let dry.
4. Position the shapes on the board and glue in place with decoupage medium. Overlap paper to cover the edges of the board.
5. Brush with two coats of decoupage medium. Let each coat dry completely.
6. Rubber stamp words with both brown and gold ink. Use lowercase letters for the large words and uppercase letters for the small words. Use a variety of pressures when stamping for a faded look. (I used EARTH, SKY, BEAUTY, CLOUDS, DREAM, HEAVEN, TREE, JOY, and SEASONS.) TIP: Since you are stamping on a coated surface, you can easily wipe off any mistakes. Remove permanent ink immediately by wiping with a damp cloth.
7. Paint the edges of the board and the pegs with undiluted raw umber. *Option:* Use a sponge brush to paint a narrow border around the edges of the board. (It's easy to make a straight line with a sponge brush. There's no need to use masking tape.) Let dry. ❑

Tuscan Landscape
vase

Although chigiri-e is Asian in origin, it's a versatile technique.
This vase, with a design inspired by the hills of Italy, would look nice
in a European country kitchen or dining room. A varnish finish is
sufficient protection if you use the vase for dried flower arrangements.
If you wish to use the vase for fresh flowers, a polymer coating is
recommended.

Pictured on page 133.

Tuscan Landscape

SUPPLIES

Base:

Ceramic vase, 4-1/4" square, 11" tall

Washi Paper:

Cream Japan Ogura (heavier, cream colored paper with long fibers)

Tools & Other Supplies:

Decoupage medium, matte finish

Paint brushes

Tube acrylic paints – Olive green, Indian red oxide, sap green, raw umber, dark blue

Copper tape, 1/4" wide, 1/2" wide

Copper metal frame embellishment with image

White craft glue

Basic supplies for washi chigiri-e (See the beginning of this section.)

Optional: Varnish in the sheen of your choice *or* polymer coating supplies (See the beginning of the Collage section for a list.)

INSTRUCTIONS

See page 131 for color examples to use as patterns.

1. Using the examples a patterns, tear the shapes from the paper.
2. Make the tree trunks by twisting 2" lengths of washi strips.
3. Using the tube acrylic paints, color the paper pieces, using the project photo as a guide:

   Sky – Leave the top strip unpainted. Color the other sky strips on the top edges with dark blue blended into white.

   Ground – Use greens with touches of red and raw umber.

   Trees and trunks – Use olive green and raw umber.
4. Position the shapes on the vase and adhere with decoupage medium, starting at the top of the vase and working down, overlapping the pieces. Feel free to modify the placement of the pieces. Wrap the top and bottom pieces of paper around the top and bottom edges of the vase to cover the rim and the bottom edge. Let dry completely.
5. Apply two more coats of decoupage medium. Let dry.
6. Affix 1/2" wide copper tape around the top rim of the vase. Using the photo as a guide, add additional strips of tape.
7. Use white craft glue to add the metal frame embellishment.
8. *Options:* Seal with varnish in the sheen of your choice *or* apply a polymer coating. See "Basic Steps for Applying a Polymer Coating" for instructions. ❏

Fields of Poppies
cards

Cut paper shapes are arranged on black card paper to make
striking floral cards. The designs can also be torn from
washi paper for chigiri-e flowers.
The flowers would also look wonderful on a coat rack, tray, or frame
with a dark basecoat. Using heavier, opaque washi paper
allows you to paste the shapes on a dark background without
losing the brilliant hues. If your base is light-colored, you can use
the thinner white unryu washi paper.

SUPPLIES

Bases:
Light green card, 5-1/2" square (folded size) and 5" x 8" (folded size)

Papers:
Black panels, 5-1/4" square and 4-1/2" x 7-1/2"
Washi paper – Japan Ogura, jute fibers (heavier, light tan colored paper with golden fibers)

Tools & Other Supplies:
Tube acrylic paints – Green light, sap green, cadmium scarlet, Payne's gray
Nori paste *or* decoupage medium
Double-sided tape
Basic supplies for washi chigiri-e and kiri-e (See the beginning of this section.)

INSTRUCTIONS

The instructions are the same for both cards.
1. Cut the shapes from washi paper, using the example for the patterns.
2. With tube acrylics, color the paper pieces, using the project photo as a guide:
Poppy – Shade the petals with scarlet on the outside edges, blending into white.
Leaves – Use a tiny amount of scarlet in the leaves along with the green hues. Let dry.
3. Position the shapes on the black panel, allowing them to overhang the edges of the panels, and adhere with nori paste. Let dry. Use the photo as a guide for placement or "grow" your own flower designs.
Option: Use decoupage medium to adhere the pieces and coat the finished cards. Let dry.
4. Trim the edges of the paper pieces flush with the edges of the panel.
5. Mount the black panel on the front of the card with double-sided tape. ❑

Pretty Pansies
cards

Pansy colors – blues, violets, and yellows – make a striking contrast when arranged on black card paper. These cut designs can also be torn from washi paper for chigiri-e flowers.
Using heavier, opaque washi paper allows you to paste the shapes on a dark background without losing the brilliant hues. If your base is light-colored, you can use the thinner white unryu washi paper.

SUPPLIES

Bases:
Yellow card, 5-1/2" square (folded size)
Dark blue card, 5" x 6-1/2" (folded size)

Papers:
Black card panels, 5-1/4" square and 4-1/2" x 6"
Washi paper – Japan Ogura, jute fibers (heavier, light tan colored paper with golden fibers)

Tools & Other Supplies:
Shimmering watercolors – Lavender, dark blue, lime green, dark green, yellow
Nori paste *or* decoupage medium
Double-sided tape
Basic supplies for washi chigiri-e and kiri-e (See the beginning of this section.)

INSTRUCTIONS

The instructions are the same for both cards.
1. Cut the shapes from washi paper, using the example for the patterns.
2. With watercolors, color the paper pieces, using the project photo as a guide.
   Pansy petals – Pansy petals come in a wide range of colors. The photo shows how different they can look even when you use the same color palette. TIP: Look at real pansies for inspiration.
   Leaves – Use greens and yellows.
   Let dry.
3. Position the shapes on the black panel, allowing them to overhang the edges of the panels, and adhere with nori paste. Use the photo as a guide for placement or "grow" your own designs. Let dry. *Option:* Use decoupage medium to adhere the pieces and coat the finished cards. Let dry.
4. Trim the edges of the paper pieces flush with the edges of the panel.
5. Mount the black panel on the front of the card with double-sided tape. ❏

Pansy Pattern

(Enlarge 135% for actual size)

Bamboo Garden
glass plate

This example of washi painting is done on a glass surface. The shapes are added to the back of the glass plate in reverse order. A large piece of washi is added last to provide a translucent background and to protect the paper design.
The delicate bamboo leaves and stalks suit the cut (kiri-e) technique, rather than chigiri-e. The design could also adorn a light-colored card, vase, or tray.

SUPPLIES

Base: Clear glass plate, 10" diameter

Washi Paper: White unryu

Tools & Other Supplies:
Decoupage medium, matte finish
Paint brushes
Tube acrylic paints – Olive green, sap green, raw umber, gray
Inkpad with permanent black ink
Rubber stamp – Asian characters
Sandpaper, 100 grit
Basic supplies for washi chigiri-e and kiri-e (See the beginning of this section.)

INSTRUCTIONS

1. Cut a circle 11" diameter from washi paper. Set aside.
2. Cut the bamboo shapes from the washi paper, using the examples as the patterns. Cut out about 30 leaves, eight to 10 large stalks, and eight to 10 small stalks.
3. Using tube acrylics, color the leaves and stalks, making the shapes a variety of shades from dark to light.
4. Position the shapes on the back of the plate and adhere with decoupage medium, placing the darker (foreground) pieces and ending with the lighter (background) pieces.

5. Color the washi circle, shading it with light gray at the edges and allowing the center to remain white. Let dry completely.

6. Using the rubber stamp and black ink, stamp Asian characters on the washi circle.

7. Adhere the circle to the back of the plate with decoupage medium, right side down. Let dry.

8. Rub the edges with sandpaper to remove the excess paper and create a smooth edge. ❏

Cherry Blossoms
plate & card

Here, the same image is used to create two different projects to show
how the same design can be applied to different surfaces.

Cherry Blossom Plate

SUPPLIES

Base:
Wooden plate, 8" diameter

Paper:
Washi paper – white unryu

Tools & Other Supplies:
Paint brushes

Shimmering watercolors – Green,
lime green, dark pink, light pink

Sandpaper, 100 grit

Decoupage medium, matte finish

Basic supplies for washi chigiri-e
(See the beginning of this section.)

Instructions begin on page 142.

Cherry Blossom Plate, continued

INSTRUCTIONS

1. Using the examples as the patterns, tear the shapes from washi paper.
2. Make the stems by twisting various lengths of washi strips.
3. Using the watercolors, color the paper pieces, using the project photo as a guide. Do not paint the pieces solidly – simply color along the top of each petal with pink paint and let the color bleed to create the shaded effect. TIP: Add a bit of the pink flower color to the green leaf color to mute the hue and give depth to the leaf.
4. Cut a 9" circle of plain washi.
5. Color the washi circle with blue at the edges, allowing the center to remain white. Let dry completely.
6. Position the circle on the front of the plate and adhere with decoupage medium.
7. Position the flower, stem, and leaf shapes on the paper surface and adhere with decoupage medium. Let dry.
8. Sand the edges to remove the excess paper and create a smooth edge. ❑

Cherry Blossom Card

Pictured on page 141

SUPPLIES

Base:

Ivory card with deckle edge, 5-1/4" x 6-3/4" (folded size)

Papers:

Ivory panel, 4" x 5-1/2"

Yuzen printed origami paper panel, 6" square

Washi paper – white unryu

Tools & Other Supplies:

Paint brushes

Shimmering watercolors – Green, lime green, dark pink, light pink

Inkpads – Brown, black

Rubber stamp – Asian characters

Glue stick

Basic supplies for washi chigiri-e (See the beginning of this section.)

INSTRUCTIONS

1. Using the example on page 140 as the patterns, tear the shapes from washi paper. Make the patterns 60% size. If you like, vary the petal shape or leaf shapes to create slightly different flowers.
2. Make the stems by twisting various lengths of washi strips.
3. Using the watercolors, color the paper pieces, using the project photo as a guide. Do not paint the pieces solidly – simply color along the top of each petal with pink paint and let the color bleed to create the shaded effect. TIP: Add a bit of the pink flower color to the green leaf color to mute the hue and give depth to the leaf.
4. Position the shapes on the ivory panel and adhere with decoupage medium. Let dry.
5. Use both black and brown inks and stamp the Asian characters, using the photo as a guide for placement. (You could use either a horizontal or vertical arrangement.)
6. Glue the printed panel to the card front. (It will frame the cherry blossom panel.) Glue the cherry blossom panel on top. ❑

Metric Conversion Chart

Inches to Millimeters and Centimeters

Inches	MM	CM	Inches	MM	CM
1/8	3	.3	2	51	5.1
1/4	6	.6	3	76	7.6
3/8	10	1.0	4	102	10.2
1/2	13	1.3	5	127	12.7
5/8	16	1.6	6	152	15.2
3/4	19	1.9	7	178	17.8
7/8	22	2.2	8	203	20.3
1	25	2.5	9	229	22.9
1-1/4	32	3.2	10	254	25.4
1-1/2	38	3.8	11	279	27.9
1-3/4	44	4.4	12	305	30.5

Yards to Meters

Yards	Meters	Yards	Meters
1/8	.11	3	2.74
1/4	.23	4	3.66
3/8	.34	5	4.57
1/2	.46	6	5.49
5/8	.57	7	6.40
3/4	.69	8	7.32
7/8	.80	9	8.23
1	.91	10	9.14
2	1.83		

Index

Index

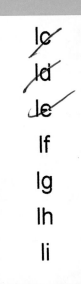